Physical Science

REINFORCEMENT & VOCABULARY REVIEW WORKSHEETS

This book was printed with soy-based ink on acid-free recycled content paper, containing 10% POSTCONSUMER WASTE.

HOLT, RINEHART AND WINSTON

A Harcourt Classroom Education Company

Austin • New York • Orlando • Atlanta • San Francisco • Boston • Dallas • Toronto • London

To the Teacher

These worksheets are designed to help you reinforce the vocabulary and concepts students need to build a solid foundation in the sciences. Key concepts are reviewed in the Reinforcement Worksheets. Key terms are stressed in the Vocabulary Review Worksheets. This booklet contains one Vocabulary Review Worksheet and at least one Reinforcement Worksheet for each chapter in the *Holt Science and Technology* Pupil's Edition.

■ REINFORCEMENT WORKSHEETS

By approaching a topic that is discussed in the Pupil's Edition from a different angle, such as with visual aids or within the framework of a new scenario, these worksheets help move students from frustration to understanding. You can use Reinforcement Worksheets to do the following:
- target the students in the class who are struggling to understand a concept;
- gauge how well the class is understanding a topic before you formally assess the topic or before you move on to a new, progressive topic;
- provide a refresher of a topic discussed in the last class period;
- conclude a lesson by having students revisit and reinforce an essential topic;
- instill confidence as students complete these enjoyable and doable worksheets;
- provide opportunities for group work and cooperative learning.

■ VOCABULARY REVIEW WORKSHEETS

With puzzles, crosswords, word searches, and other nonintimidating challenges, the Vocabulary Review Worksheets can help your students do the following:
- remember important vocabulary terms from each chapter;
- review and study vocabulary definitions;
- think critically about the way in which the words are used in talking about science;
- warm up for a new lesson by starting out with a puzzle;
- participate in cooperative learning activities by solving puzzles with a partner or group.

ANSWER KEY

For your convenience, an answer key is provided in the back of this booklet. The key includes reduced versions of all applicable worksheets with answers included.

Art and Photo Credits
All work, unless otherwise noted, contributed by Holt, Rinehart and Winston.
Abbreviated as follows: (t) top; (b) bottom; (l) left; (r) right; (c) center; (bkgd) background.
Front cover (owl), Kim Taylor/Bruce Coleman, Inc.; (bridge), Henry K. Kaiser/Leo de Wys; (dove), Stephen Dalton/Photo Researchers, Inc.; Page 57 (tr), Tom Galgliano; 68 (b), Tom Galgliano; 77 (tr), Carlyn Iverson; 81 (r), Tom Galgliano

Printed in the United States of America

ISBN 0-03-055412-8   1 2 3 4 5 6 085 04 03 02 01 00

· CONTENTS ·

CONTENTS, CONTINUED

CONTENTS, CONTINUED

CHAPTER

1 | **REINFORCEMENT WORKSHEET**

The Plane Truth

Complete this worksheet after you finish reading Chapter 1, Section 2.

You plan to enter a paper airplane contest sponsored by *Talkin' Physical Science* magazine. The person whose airplane flies the farthest wins a lifetime subscription to the magazine! The week before the contest, you watch an airplane landing at a nearby airport. You notice that the wings of the airplane have flaps, as shown in the illustration at right. The paper airplanes you've been testing do not have wing flaps.

What question would you ask yourself based on these observations? Write your question in the space below for "State the problem." Then tell how you could use the other steps in the scientific method to investigate the problem.

1. State the problem.

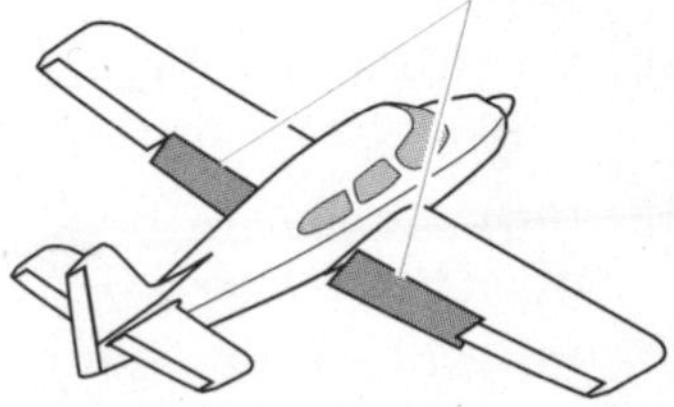

_____

_____

Flaps

2. Form a hypothesis.

_____

_____

3. Test the hypothesis.

_____

_____

_____

_____

4. Analyze the results.

_____

_____

_____

5. Draw conclusions.

_____

_____

_____

_____

CHAPTER
1 **VOCABULARY REVIEW WORKSHEET**

The Wide World of Physical Science

After finishing Chapter 1, give this puzzle a try!

ACROSS

1. the ratio of an object's mass to its volume
2. the amount of space something occupies
3. any use of the senses to gather information
4. the application of knowledge, tools, and materials to accomplish tasks
6. measure of the amount of matter in an object
10. Scientists use the _____ System of Units so they can share and compare results.
13. measure of how much surface an object has
15. measure of how hot or cold something is
16. The study of matter and energy is called _____ science.

DOWN

1. A quantity formed from the combination of other measurements is a _____ quantity.
5. a possible explanation or answer to a question
6. A representation of a salt crystal made out of table-tennis balls is a _____ of the crystal.
7. Scientists use the _____ method to solve problems and answer questions.
8. an experimental boat that imitates the way a penguin swims
9. in science, a summary of many experimental results and observations
11. a scientific explanation for a range of hypotheses and observations supported by testing
12. pieces of information acquired through experimentation
14. the basic SI unit of length

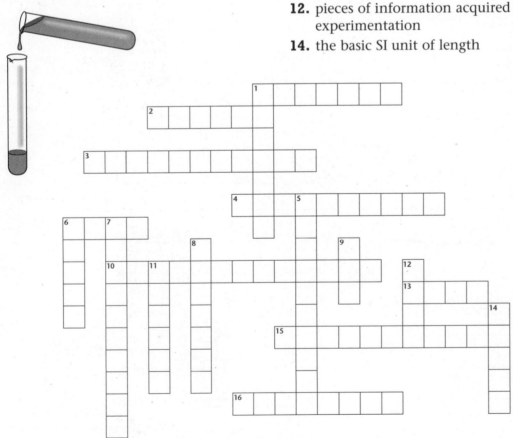

Name _____ Date _____ Class _____

A Matter of Density

Complete this worksheet after you finish reading Chapter 2, Section 2.

Imagine that you work at a chemical plant. This morning, four different liquid chemicals accidentally spilled into the same tank. Luckily, none of the liquids reacted with each other! Also, you know the liquids do not dissolve in one another, so they must have settled in the tank in four separate layers. The sides of the tank are made of steel, so you can only see the surface of what's inside. But you need to remove the red chemical to use in a reaction later this afternoon. How will you find and remove the red chemical? By finding the chemicals' different densities, of course!

The following liquids were spilled into the tank:

- a green liquid that has a volume of 48 L and a mass of 36 kg
- a blue liquid that has a volume of 144 L and a mass of 129.6 kg
- a red liquid that has a volume of 96 L and a mass of 115.2 kg
- a black liquid that has a volume of 120 L and a mass of 96 kg

1. Calculate the density of each liquid.

Green liquid: _____

Blue liquid: _____

Red liquid: _____

Black liquid: _____

2. Determine the order in which the liquids have settled in the tank.

First (bottom): _____

Second: _____

Third: _____

Fourth (top): _____

3. Use colored pencils to sketch the liquid layers in the container in the diagram on the next page.

4. What kind of property did you use to distinguish between these four chemicals?
  a. a chemical property
  b. a physical property
  c. a liquid property
  d. None of the above

A Matter of Density, continued

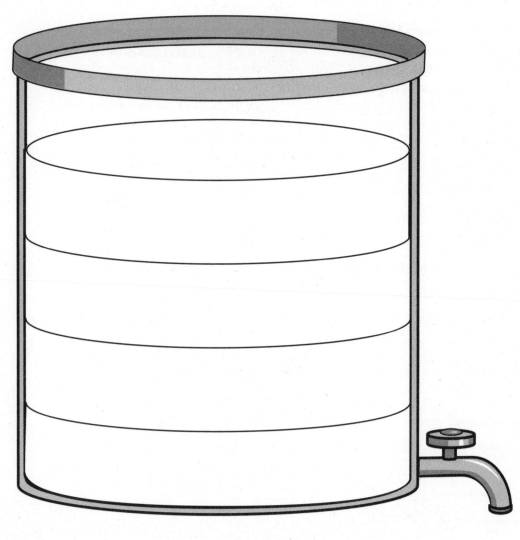

5. Now that you know where the red chemical is inside the tank, how can you remove it?

_____

_____

_____

_____

CHAPTER

2 VOCABULARY REVIEW WORKSHEET

Search for Matter

Complete the puzzle after you finish reading Chapter 2.

Fill in each blank with the correct word. Then find the words in the puzzle. Words in the puzzle can be spelled forward or backward and can be vertical, horizontal, or diagonal.

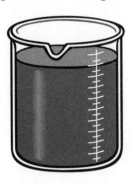

1. The tendency of an object to resist any change in motion is called

_____ .

2. When water is in a container, the surface of the water is curved. This curve is

called the _____ .

3. The amount of space occupied by an object

is its _____ .

4. Iron _____ is also known as fool's gold.

5. The _____ of an object is the amount of matter in the object. The SI unit for expressing this quantity is

the _____ .

6. The force that causes an object to feel a "pull" toward Earth is

called _____ . The measure of this force is

the object's _____ . The SI unit for

expressing this force is the _____ .

7. _____ is anything that has volume and mass.

8. _____ is mass divided by unit volume.

9. A _____ change occurs when one or more substances are changed into entirely new substances with different properties.

10. Examples of _____ properties are color and odor.

11. A _____ property is always the same, whether the sample observed is large or small.

Search for Matter, continued

W	P	F	X	D	E	N	S	I	T	Y	E	P	C
R	E	V	Q	C	J	N	D	Q	W	M	I	I	J
B	P	I	N	E	W	T	O	N	U	A	T	G	K
A	E	F	G	E	X	J	O	L	N	S	I	K	I
G	X	C	J	H	H	P	O	D	I	I	I	K	L
R	Y	M	H	R	T	V	V	R	C	N	Q	P	O
A	S	A	K	E	T	S	E	M	A	E	X	H	G
V	T	S	L	D	M	T	N	F	M	R	U	Y	R
I	W	S	N	N	C	I	M	V	X	T	Z	S	A
T	Y	U	K	A	C	G	C	A	X	I	N	I	M
Y	O	D	R	J	I	N	T	A	T	A	Q	C	M
P	T	A	P	Y	R	I	T	E	L	T	R	A	W
C	H	Z	M	M	P	V	Q	P	B	Z	E	L	B
C	T	Z	C	M	E	N	I	S	C	U	S	R	P

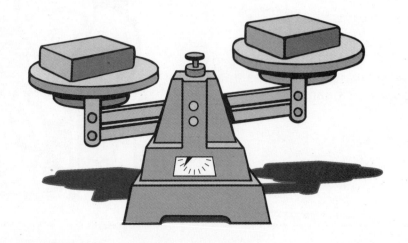

Name ______________________ Date ______________ Class ______________

CHAPTER 3 REINFORCEMENT WORKSHEET

Make a State-ment

Complete this worksheet after you finish reading Chapter 3, Section 2.
Each figure below shows a container that is meant to hold one state of matter. Identify the state of matter, and write the state on the line below the corresponding figure. Then write each of the descriptions listed below in the correct boxes. Some descriptions may go in more than one box.

Particles are close together.

Particles are held tightly in place by other particles.

Particles break away completely from one another.

changes volume to fill its container

changes shape when placed in a different container

can be used in hydraulic systems

obeys Boyle's law

amount of empty space can change

has definite shape

particles vibrate in place

does not change in volume

has surface tension

State of matter	Description
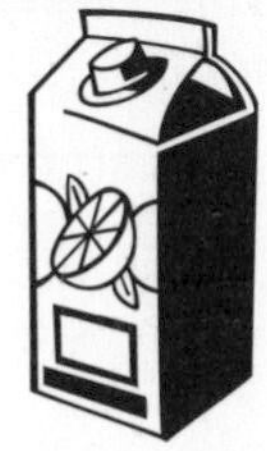 ______________	
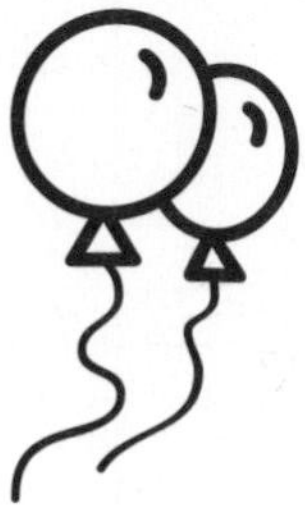 ______________	
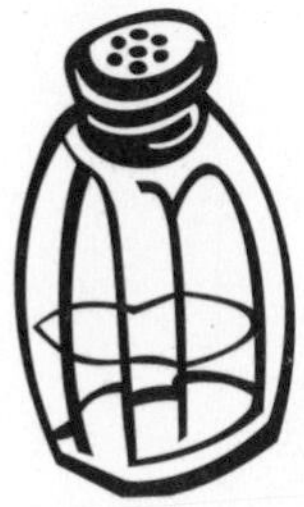 ______________	

CHAPTER

3 **VOCABULARY REVIEW WORKSHEET**

Know Your States

After you finish Chapter 3, give this puzzle a try!
Use the clues below to complete the crossword puzzle.

ACROSS

3. to change state from a gas to a liquid

6. change of state from a solid to a gas

7. Particles have an orderly arrangement in this type of solid.

10. physical form in which a substance can exist

11. how your body is cooled when you perspire

14. changes shape but doesn't change volume

15. He said that as the volume of a gas increases, its pressure decreases.

16. how molten metal changes into a solid

18. does not change shape when placed in a different container

DOWN

1. measure of the average speed of the particles of a substance

2. to change state from a solid to a liquid

4. Because of surface tension liquids form spherical _____ .

5. has no definite shape or volume; conducts electric current

8. Particles are arranged in no particular order in this type of solid.

9. A change of state where energy is given off is called a(n) _____ change.

12. If a substance pours very slowly, it has a high _____ .

13. A change of state reaction that _____ energy is endothermic.

15. how hot water changes to steam

17. changes shape and volume to fit container

Name _____ Date _____ Class _____

It's All Mixed Up

Complete this worksheet after you finish reading Chapter 4, Section 3.

Label each figure below with the type of substance it BEST models:
colloid, compound, element, solution, or suspension.

1.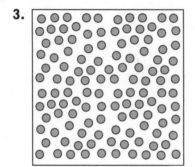

_____

2.

_____

3.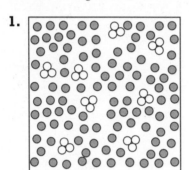

_____

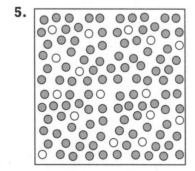

4.

_____

5.

_____

6. Why did you label the figures on the previous page as you did?

_____

_____

_____

_____

_____

_____

_____

_____

_____

_____

Professor Jumble's Confusion

In her lab, Professor Jumble has four shelves labeled "Suspensions," "Solutions," "Compounds," and "Colloids," respectively. Last night, the professor set one beaker of clear liquid on each of the four shelves. When the professor walked into her lab this morning, all four beakers were on the same shelf, and she didn't know which was which. She tested each beaker, and the results are below.

Use the test results to help Professor Jumble unjumble the beakers, and write the identity of each liquid in the blanks.

Beaker A: _____	Beaker B: _____
• Light passes right through. • Particles do not separate in a centrifuge or a filter. • Upon heating, the liquid evaporates, and a crystal powder remains.	• Light passes right through. • Particles do not separate in a centrifuge or a filter. • Upon heating, the liquid evaporates, but no residue remains. • The particles could not be separated by any other physical changes.
Beaker C: _____	Beaker D: _____
• Liquid scatters light. • Liquid centrifuged into two different-colored layers. • Particles were left behind in the filter.	• Liquid scatters light. • Liquid passes through a filter without leaving a residue.

CHAPTER
4 **VOCABULARY REVIEW WORKSHEET**

An ELEMENTary Word Puzzle

Give this puzzle a try after you read Chapter 4.

Identify each term described by the clues. Then find and circle each term in the puzzle on the next page. Words may appear forward or backward, horizontally, vertically, or diagonally.

1. _____ amount of solute needed to make a saturated solution using a given amount of solvent at a certain temperature

2. _____ mixture in which dispersed particles are too light to settle out

3. _____ substance in which another is dissolved

4. _____ can be expressed as grams of solute per milliliter of solvent

5. _____ pure substance that cannot be separated into simpler substances by physical or chemical means

6. _____ two or more substances that are combined physically, not chemically

7. _____ pure substance made up of at least two elements that are chemically combined

8. _____ characteristic property measured in grams per cubic centimeter that tells a substance's mass per unit volume

9. _____ element that has properties of both metals and nonmetals

10. _____ solid solution of a metal or a nonmetal dissolved in a metal

11. _____ dissolved substance

12. _____ shiny element; good conductor of thermal energy and electric current

13. _____ mixture in which particles of one substance are large enough to settle out of another substance

14. _____ brass, salt water, and air, for example

15. _____ element that is a poor conductor of thermal energy and electric current

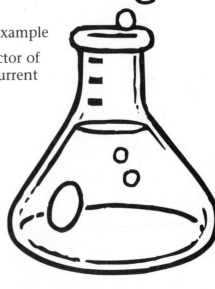

An ELEMENTary Word Puzzle, continued

F	S	O	L	U	B	I	L	I	T	Y	L	O	Z	F
S	J	O	H	E	C	U	F	L	A	M	T	Y	E	C
O	K	I	L	T	N	E	M	E	L	E	B	I	H	O
D	O	P	R	U	N	E	T	R	O	J	I	N	S	N
E	I	M	E	L	T	Z	R	N	I	O	P	M	O	C
N	M	O	N	A	C	E	O	P	C	S	J	D	A	E
S	S	O	L	V	E	N	T	G	O	N	U	N	R	N
I	D	N	E	L	P	S	W	L	L	P	S	U	C	T
T	X	R	S	Y	A	V	U	A	L	M	T	O	A	R
Y	E	U	K	C	S	T	T	A	O	X	D	P	R	A
O	T	P	U	R	I	E	E	P	I	A	E	M	B	T
L	A	M	X	O	M	S	N	M	D	V	J	O	A	I
L	W	K	N	N	K	C	R	E	D	E	M	C	T	O
A	L	O	O	L	S	U	S	P	E	N	S	I	O	N
E	N	N	A	R	A	H	C	B	O	Z	L	T	U	Q

CHAPTER

5 REINFORCEMENT WORKSHEET

Bug Race

Complete this worksheet after you finish reading Chapter 5, Section 1.
You and a friend are having a bug race. You measure the distance your pet bugs travel along a straight race track and record their time as they race. The results are plotted in the graphs below. Take a look at the two graphs. Then answer the questions that follow.

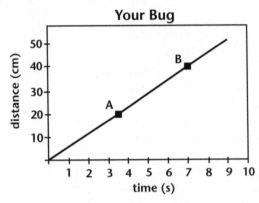

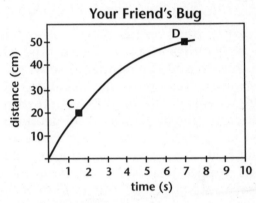

1. Look at Point A. What distance has your bug traveled so far? _____

2. How long did it take your bug to travel that distance? _____

3. To determine your bug's average speed while traveling from the starting line to Point A, divide the distance traveled by the time it took to travel that distance:

   $$\text{average speed} = \frac{\text{distance traveled}}{\text{elapsed time}} = \text{\underline{\hspace{5cm}}}$$

4. Now look at Point B. What is the distance from Point A to Point B? _____

5. How long did it take your bug to travel from Point A to Point B? _____

6. Calculate your bug's average speed from Point A to Point B.

   _____

7. Compare the graphs of your bug and your friend's bug. Which bug was traveling at a constant speed? Explain.

   _____

   _____

   _____

   _____

CHAPTER

5 **REINFORCEMENT WORKSHEET**

Friction Action

Complete this worksheet after you finish reading Chapter 5, Section 3.

Steve challenged his little sister Jenny to a problem: Use all four types of friction to get home from school as quickly and as safely as possible. He reminded her that the four types of friction are sliding, rolling, static, and fluid. Here's what Jenny did:

Jenny hopped on her bicycle after school. What a perfect day to be cycling—the sun was shining, there was a slight breeze in the air, and the temperature was a comfortable 27°C. Jenny got on the bike path and began pedaling as fast as she could. The wheels of the bicycle were turning at a furious pace. And the faster Jenny pedaled, the stronger the breezy air blew in her face. All of a sudden, she came across a huge tree branch that had fallen on the path. Jenny slammed on her brakes and stopped just in time to avoid hitting the fallen branch. That was a close call! She got off of her bike and tried to push the branch to the side of the path so that others would not get hurt, but it was too heavy to budge. Jenny continued on her journey and got home safely in record time.

Did Jenny meet Steve's challenge? Explain.

_____

_____

_____

_____

_____

_____

_____

_____

_____

CHAPTER

5 **REINFORCEMENT WORKSHEET**

A Weighty Problem

Complete this worksheet after you finish reading Chapter 5, Section 4.

Pictured below are two measurement devices, *A* and *B*.

Weight or Mass?	Weight or Mass?

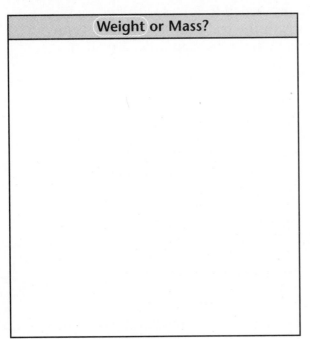

A.

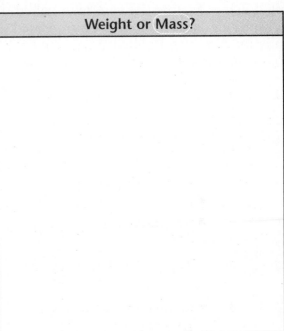

B.

1. Determine whether each device measures *mass* or *weight,* and circle the correct term in each box.

2. The following list contains information that relates to either *mass* or *weight.* Write each of the bulleted items in the correct boxes above. Some information may go in more than one box.

- balance
- spring scale
- measure of gravitational force exerted on an object
- amount of matter in an object
- constant on Earth
- measured in grams

- changes when gravitational force changes
- never changes
- expressed in newtons
- remains the same when gravitational force changes
- six times less on the moon than on Earth

CHAPTER
5 VOCABULARY REVIEW WORKSHEET

Penny's Puns

After you finish Chapter 5, give this puzzle a try!

Oh no! Penny Punster's computer mixed up her physical science dictionary with her dictionary of puns. The computer paired the terms related to forces with her goofy definitions, and it paired her pun-related terms with the real definitions. Help Penny unscramble the mismatched pairs and get her dictionaries back in order. The first one has been done for you!

__c__ **1. farce:** a push or pull

_____ **2. grubby tea:** force of attraction between objects due to mass

_____ **3. freak sheen:** force opposing motion between touching surfaces

_____ **4. fellow's city:** speed in a particular direction

_____ **5. sty tic:** friction that disappears when an object starts moving

_____ **6. exhilaration:** rate at which velocity changes

_____ **7. mow shun:** changing position over time

_____ **8. spyed:** rate at which an object moves

_____ **9. bell lanced:** forces producing a net force of zero

_____ **10. net for us:** result of combined forces on an object

_____ **11. wade:** measure of the force of gravity on an object

_____ **12. mace:** amount of matter in an object

_____ **13. roe link:** friction between wheels and the floor

_____ **14. Libra can't:** reduces friction

_____ **15. flu ad:** friction that slows down a swimmer

_____ **16. now ten:** unit used to express force

_____ **17. sly ding:** friction that makes brakes work

a. balanced: a ringer on a stick

b. newton: used to be nine

c. force: slapstick

d. fluid: influenza commercial

e. motion: lawn-cutting avoidance

f. gravity: dirty English drink

g. velocity: guy's town

h. net force: mesh that's ours

i. static: pigpen twitch

j. mass: spiked medieval war club

k. friction: weird shininess

l. acceleration: thrill

m. weight: slowly walk into the water

n. speed: played secret agent

o. sliding: sneaky dent

p. lubricant: the sign between Virgo and Scorpio won't work

q. rolling: fish egg connection

_____ Date _____ Class _____

you finish reading **Chapter 6, Section 1.**

e partially completed table below
velocity of the stone for the first

late the velocity of the stone at the
that acceleration due to gravity is
the answers in the table in the column labeled
"Velocity." The first few calculations are done for you.

Notice that the stone's initial velocity is 0 m/s. The velocity at
the end of one second is the initial velocity plus the change in
velocity due to gravity:

velocity = initial velocity + change in velocity

Since the initial velocity is 0 m/s, we can ignore it.
velocity = change in velocity
= Δv
= (acceleration due to gravity) × (time)

Time (s)	Velocity (m/s)	Distance fallen during this second (m)
0	0	0
1	$\Delta v = 9.8 \times 1 = 9.8$	4.9
2	$\Delta v = 9.8 \times 2 = 19.6$	4.9 + 9.8 = 14.7
3		4.9 + 9.8 + 9.8 = 24.5
4		4.9 + 3(9.8) = 34.3
5		
6		

2. Do you see the pattern in the calculations for the third column?
Calculate the distance fallen in each second, and record the two
remaining values in the column labeled "Distance fallen during
this second" in the table.

Falling Fast, continued

3. After 2 seconds, the stone will have fallen a total of 19.6 m (distance after first second + distance during second second). How far will the stone have fallen after 5 seconds? (Use the space below for your calculations.)

After 5 seconds, the stone will have fallen

_____ m.

4. Approximately when will the stone hit the ground? Explain your reasoning.

_____

_____

_____

_____

_____

_____

_____

_____

5. If a much heavier stone rolled off the same cliff, would it hit the ground more quickly? Explain.

_____

_____

_____

_____

CHAPTER
6 **VOCABULARY REVIEW WORKSHEET**

A Matter of Real Gravity

After you finish Chapter 6, give this puzzle a try!

Use the clues given to fill in the blanks below. Then copy the numbered letters into the corresponding squares on the next page to reveal a quotation attributed to Galileo.

1. When gravity is the only force acting on an object, the object is in

___ ___ ___ ___   ___ ___ ___ ___ .
52   47   29

2. Because of free fall, astronauts appear this way in orbit.

___ ___ ___ ___ ___ ___ ___ ___ ___ ___
   40   51 2 13   44

3. The velocity at which a falling object travels when the force of air resistance exactly matches the downward force of gravity is called the

___ ___ ___ ___ ___   ___ ___ ___ ___ ___ ___ ___ .
12   46   17 25   8   19   49 30

4. The unbalanced force that causes an object to move in a circular path is called a _____ force.

___ ___ ___ ___ ___ ___ ___ ___ ___ ___
32   22   42 1   39

5. Sir Isaac Newton is famous for his three laws of

___ ___ ___ ___ ___ ___ .
11 54 38   33 26

6. Newton's third law states that objects exert _____ and _____ forces on each other.

___ ___ ___ ___ ___   ___ ___ ___ ___ ___ ___
       34 16   23 18 31

7. The curved path traveled by a thrown baseball is known as

___ ___ ___ ___ ___ ___ ___ ___ ___ ___ ___ ___ ___ .
   10 45   27   35   15 37   6

8. The acceleration of a falling object is caused by the force of

___ ___ ___ ___ ___ ___ .
21 53   4   48

9. _____ is the tendency of an object to resist any change in its motion.

___ ___ ___ ___ ___ ___ ___
   50   24   56 3

10. A moving object's _____ depends on the object's mass and velocity.

___ ___ ___ ___ ___ ___ ___ ___
55   9 43   57

11. The fluid friction that opposes the motion of objects through air
is known as

$\overline{}_{14}$ $\overline{}$ $\overline{}$ $\quad$ $\overline{}$ $\overline{}_{5}$ $\overline{}$ $\overline{}_{20}$ $\overline{}$ $\overline{}_{28}$ $\overline{}_{41}$ $\overline{}_{36}$ $\overline{}$ $\overline{}_{7}$.

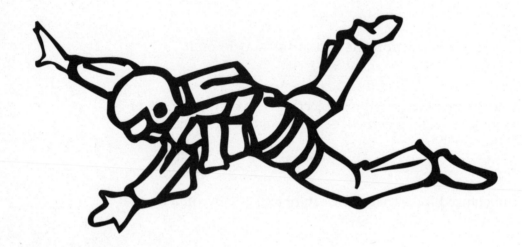

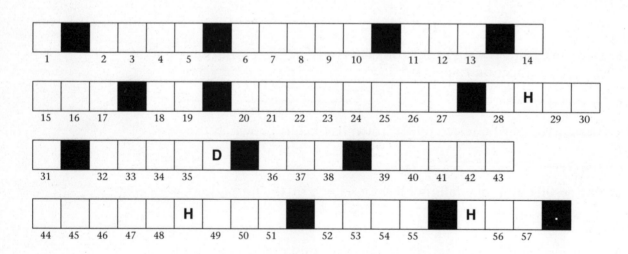

CHAPTER

7 **REINFORCEMENT WORKSHEET**

Building Up Pressure

Complete this worksheet after you finish reading Chapter 7.

1. Below is a diagram of a balloon that has just been released. Identify the areas of high and low pressure, and label them on the diagram.

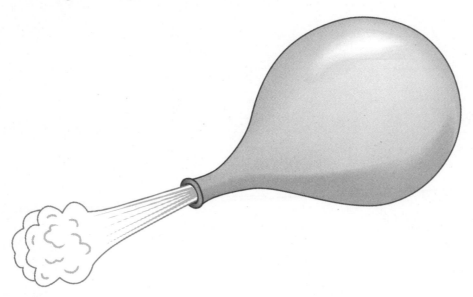

2. Why does air rush out of the balloon when you release it?

_____

_____

_____

_____

_____

_____

_____

_____

3. Is the pressure of the stream of air exiting the balloon different from the pressure of the air around the balloon? Explain in terms of Bernoulli's principle.

_____

_____

_____

_____

_____

_____

_____

_____

4. Add an arrow to the diagram on the previous page to show the direction of the air coming out of the balloon. Add another arrow indicating the direction the balloon is pushed by the exiting air. Label the first arrow "Air outflow," and label the second arrow "Thrust."

5. If you attach some weight to the balloon, it might not be able to fly. Use the terms *weight, thrust,* and *lift* to explain.

_____

_____

_____

_____

_____

_____

_____

_____

CHAPTER

7 VOCABULARY REVIEW WORKSHEET

Go with the Flow

After completing Chapter 7, give this puzzle a try!
Fill in the blanks in the clues below. Then use the clues to complete the puzzle on the next page.

Clues

1. _____ discovered that the buoyant force depends on the weight of the displaced fluid.

2. _____ described the connection between fluid speed and pressure.

3. A swim _____ controls a fish's overall density.

4. _____ force is the upward force exerted on any object in a fluid.

5. The layer of gases surrounding the Earth is called the

   _____ .

6. A _____ is something that flows.

7. _____ is the upward force due to fluid flow around an airplane wing.

8. The amount of matter in a certain volume divided by the volume

   is _____ .

9. A fluid force that opposes motion is called

   _____ .

10. One newton per square meter is a _____ .

11. A _____ device uses a liquid to transmit pressure from one point to another.

12. An irregular fluid flow is _____ .

13. To _____ is to move into something else's location by pushing it aside.

14. _____ is the amount of force exerted on a given area divided by the area.

15. The forward force from a plane's engine is _____ .

How many chapter concepts can you find in the block of letters below? Use the clues on the previous page to help you. Words may appear horizontally, vertically, diagonally, or backward.

T	U	R	B	U	L	E	N	C	E	M	E	Z	C	E	E	K
C	A	S	O	Q	V	H	Y	D	R	A	U	L	I	C	D	I
P	R	E	S	S	U	R	E	G	Y	Q	A	K	J	E	X	Q
O	Z	D	Q	G	R	T	N	A	Y	O	U	B	S	B	R	Z
B	K	D	F	P	D	E	N	S	I	T	Y	S	S	L	K	I
T	P	C	H	D	G	C	T	P	X	T	E	E	J	A	Z	J
A	S	J	A	W	B	N	S	G	T	R	D	R	Z	D	F	D
O	T	U	A	J	A	F	G	F	P	E	S	X	M	D	S	Z
G	I	M	R	Z	Z	Q	I	M	M	J	C	X	S	E	U	I
S	E	V	O	H	T	L	O	I	B	H	T	M	C	R	D	L
Q	P	L	B	S	T	C	H	L	H	B	B	J	P	G	I	L
X	Y	R	W	G	P	C	I	O	N	F	T	D	A	J	S	U
U	R	M	N	D	R	H	I	S	F	F	U	A	S	I	P	O
C	T	T	I	A	R	E	D	N	J	J	A	C	F	L	N
Q	M	U	V	Q	A	R	J	R	R	W	H	R	A	P	A	R
V	L	L	H	U	Y	R	M	W	E	A	R	R	L	P	C	E
F	Q	J	F	I	M	F	J	O	U	H	G	F	S	L	E	B

Mechanical Advantage and Efficiency

Complete this worksheet after you have finished reading Chapter 8, Section 3.

Carlita, Tom, and Jamal are having a contest to see who can build the best pulley. After they finish constructing the pulleys, they measure the input and output forces as well as the input and output work. Below is a chart with the results. Help the three students calculate the mechanical advantage and the mechanical efficiency of each of the pulleys.

1. What is the output force of Tom's pulley? _____

2. What is the input force of Tom's pulley? _____

3. Divide the output force by the input force. _____

4. Your answer for item 3 is the mechanical advantage for Tom's pulley. Record this value on the chart below. Calculate the mechanical advantage of the other two pulleys in the same way, and record these values on the chart.

5. What is the output work of Carlita's pulley? _____

6. What is the input work of Carlita's pulley? _____

7. Divide the output work by the input work. _____

8. Multiply your answer for item 7 by 100%. _____

9. Your answer for item 8 is the mechanical efficiency for Carlita's pulley. Record this value on the chart. Calculate the mechanical efficiency of the other two pulleys in the same way, and fill in these values in the chart.

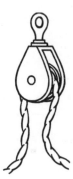

	Force (N)		Work (J)		Mechanical advantage	Mechanical efficiency
	Input	Output	Input	Output		
Carlita	4	8	4	3		
Tom	15	60	12	6		
Jamal	25	100	10	9		

10. Based on your calculations, whose pulley won the contest? Explain your reasoning.

_____

_____

_____

_____

_____

CHAPTER
8 **REINFORCEMENT WORKSHEET**

Finding Machines in Everyday Life

Complete this worksheet after you have finished reading Chapter 8, Section 3.

In Chapter 8 you learned about work and how machines can help make all kinds of work easier. You saw examples of simple machines and compound machines. In the drawing below, find as many machines as you can, and classify them as simple or compound. For each simple machine, write what type of simple machine it is.

Simple Machines   **Compound Machines**

_____   _____

_____   _____

_____   _____

_____   _____

_____   _____

_____   _____

_____   _____

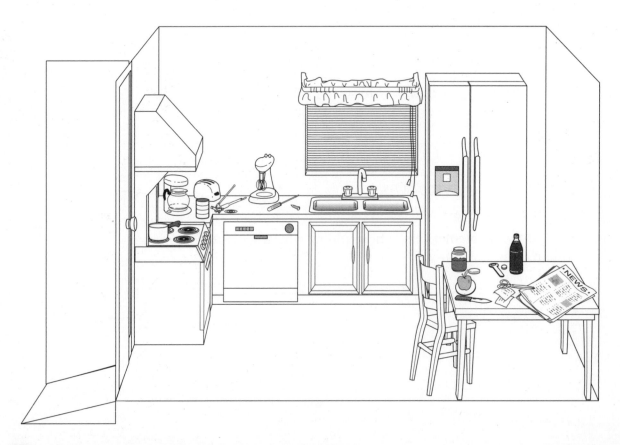

CHAPTER

8 VOCABULARY REVIEW WORKSHEET

Searching for Work

Now that you have read Chapter 8, give this word search a try!

After filling in the blanks, find the words in the puzzle on the next page.

1. The unit used to express work is the _____ .

2. A _____ is an inclined plane that is wrapped in a spiral.

3. _____ is the rate at which work is done.

4. _____ occurs when a force causes an object to move in the direction of the force.

5. The work you do on a machine is called the work _____ .

6. An _____ is a simple machine that is a straight, slanted surface.

7. The mechanical _____ of a machine compares the input force with the output force.

8. All machines are constructed from six _____ machines.

9. When two kinds of pulleys are used together, the system is called a

_____ .

10. A _____ is a simple machine consisting of a bar that pivots at a fixed point.

11. A _____ is a device that helps make work easier by changing the size or direction of force.

12. A _____ is a double inclined plane that moves.

13. Machines that are made up of two or more simple machines are called

_____ machines.

14. A _____ is a simple machine consisting of two circular objects of different sizes.

15. A _____ consists of a grooved wheel that holds a rope or a cable.

16. The work done by a machine is called the work _____ .

17. The fixed point at which a lever pivots is called a _____ .

18. Two kinds of pulleys are _____ pulleys and

_____ pulleys.

19. The unit used to express power is the _____ .

20. Mechanical _____ is a comparison of a machine's work output with the work input.

Searching for Work, continued

In the puzzle below, find the words from the blanks on the previous page. Words may appear horizontally, vertically, or diagonally.

F	B	P	B	W	A	T	T	N	C	S	K	R	E	E
F	U	L	U	Y	Q	O	U	C	M	I	E	L	N	R
E	P	L	O	L	U	E	P	C	W	V	P	A	R	W
F	C	S	C	C	L	F	H	D	E	M	L	E	E	W
F	O	A	F	R	K	E	B	L	I	P	F	M	E	E
I	M	X	I	J	U	A	Y	S	D	H	K	W	H	D
C	P	F	X	X	F	M	N	E	J	O	U	L	E	G
I	O	D	E	X	T	A	N	D	O	P	J	H	Q	E
E	U	W	D	W	S	I	E	M	T	Z	O	H	C	D
N	N	V	E	T	L	N	D	U	O	A	L	W	C	U
C	D	R	U	C	I	J	S	P	U	V	C	T	E	F
Y	C	P	N	H	O	U	T	P	U	T	A	K	D	R
S	N	I	C	W	O	R	K	X	Q	K	D	B	L	U
I	Z	A	V	A	D	V	A	N	T	A	G	E	L	E
D	M	W	H	E	E	L	A	N	D	A	X	L	E	E

See What I Saw

Complete this worksheet after you finish reading Chapter 9, Section 2.

In each of the following diagrams, a boy and a girl of equal mass sit on opposite sides of a seesaw. The arrows indicate direction of movement. Take a few moments to look over the figures, and then circle the statement that correctly describes the transfer of energy for each figure.

1.

   a. The girl's potential energy increases as the boy's kinetic energy increases.

   b. The boy's potential energy and the girl's potential energy decrease.

   c. The girl's kinetic energy increases as the boy's potential energy increases.

   d. The kinetic and potential energies of the boy and the girl are equal.

2.

   a. The girl's potential energy increases as the boy's kinetic energy increases.

   b. The boy's potential energy and the girl's potential energy decrease.

   c. The girl's kinetic energy increases as the boy's potential energy increases.

   d. The kinetic and potential energies of the boy and the girl are equal.

3.

   a. The girl's potential energy increases as the boy's kinetic energy increases.

   b. The boy's potential energy and the girl's potential energy decrease.

   c. The girl's kinetic energy increases as the boy's potential energy increases.

   d. The kinetic and potential energies of the boy and the girl are equal.

4. Remember that mechanical energy is the sum of kinetic and potential energy. What happens to the amount of mechanical energy in the boy in Figure 3 as his potential and kinetic energies change?

_____

_____

CHAPTER

9 **REINFORCEMENT WORKSHEET**

Energetic Cooking

Complete this worksheet after you finish reading Chapter 9, Section 2.

Jerry is busy preparing for breakfast. Little does he know that energy conversions are taking place every step of the way! Identify the energy conversion that takes place after each of Jerry's actions, and describe the energy conversion in the space provided.

1. Jerry dusted off his solar-powered juice maker and placed it in direct sunlight so he could make freshly squeezed orange juice to go with his breakfast.

_____

_____

2. Jerry plugged in the electric frying pan, turned it on "high," and waited a few minutes while the pan heated.

_____

_____

3. When the indicator light turned on, Jerry was ready to cook.

_____

_____

4. He mixed up his secret recipe, poured it into the pan, and listened as the mixture sizzled.

_____

_____

5. As the mixture heated, it thickened and started to change color.

_____

_____

6. When the mixture seemed cooked, Jerry placed it on his plate and turned off the frying pan. Next he added cold water to the frying pan, which made a giant "whooshing" noise.

_____

_____

BONUS QUESTION: What energy conversion takes place in Jerry's body after he eats the breakfast he has prepared?

CHAPTER
9 VOCABULARY REVIEW WORKSHEET

Exercising Your Potential

Complete the following puzzle after you finish reading Chapter 9.

Use each of the following clues to find the correct energy-related word, and write the word in the spaces provided. Then on the next page, put the numbered letters into the matching numbered squares to reveal a quotation by Nancy Newhall.

1. a force that opposes motion between surfaces that are touching

__ __ __ __ __ __ __ __
35   9

2. energy resources that formed from the buried remains of plants and animals that lived millions of years ago

__ __ __ __ __ __ __   __ __ __ __ __
14   38

3. the energy of motion

__ __ __ __ __ __ __
3   20

4. the process that captures the sun's energy for food making in plants

__ __ __ __ __ __ __ __ __ __ __ __
11   21 33   10

5. energy resources that cannot be replaced after they are used

__ __ __ __ __ __ __ __ __ __ __
19   8

6. units used to express energy

__ __ __ __ __ __
30   40

7. a well-defined group of objects that transfer energy between one another

__ __ __ __ __ __ __   __ __ __ __ __ __
1   32   17

8. the sum of kinetic and potential energies

__ __ __ __ __ __ __   __ __ __ __ __ __ __
15   18

9. potential energy dependent upon an object's weight and distance from the Earth's surface

__ __ __ __ __ __ __ __ __ __ __ __
28   7   37

10. the ability to do work

__ __ __ __ __ __
34   39

11. resources that can be used and replaced in nature over a relatively short period of time

__ __ __ __ __ __ __ __ __ __
6

12. the energy of shape or position

___ ___ ___ ___ ___ ___ ___ ___ ___
   2   13

13. a change of one form of energy into another

___ ___ ___ ___ ___ ___ ___ ___ ___ ___ ___
23   4   27

14. produced when two or more nuclei join together or when the nucleus of one atom splits apart

___ ___ ___ ___ ___ ___   ___ ___ ___ ___ ___ ___
   16   24   12

15. a natural resource that can be converted by humans into other forms of energy in order to do useful work

___ ___ ___ ___ ___ ___   ___ ___ ___ ___ ___ ___ ___ ___
          25   36   31

16. a comparison of the amount of energy before a conversion with the amount of useful energy after a conversion

___ ___ ___ ___ ___ ___
       5   22

___ ___ ___ ___ ___ ___ ___ ___ ___ ___ ___
    29   26

Nancy Newhall's Quotation:

Name _____ Date _____ Class _____

Feel the Heat

Complete this worksheet after you have finished reading Chapter 10, Section 2.

Beneath the description, write the method of heating that is taking place. (conduction, convection, or radiation)

1. One heater located in the deep end warms Carlos's entire swimming pool.

_____

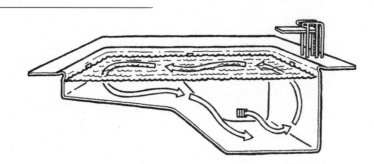

2. The sunlight shines directly on Janet's desk but not on Carlos's desk. Both Janet and Carlos are near the window, yet Janet feels much warmer than Carlos.

_____

3. Carlos places a spoon in a steaming hot bowl of soup. Minutes later, the hot handle burns his fingers.

_____

4. Carlos licks a juice pop that he has just removed from the freezer. The tip of his tongue freezes and sticks to the icy-cold treat.

_____

5. When Janet sits near the campfire, her face feels hot even though her back feels cold.

_____

6. When Janet wins first place in the science-fair competition, Carlos shakes her hand. Her hand feels cold to him.

_____

7. Bubbles of liquid in Carlos's lava lamp are heated at the lamp's base. The bubbles then rise to the top. They fall after being cooled.

_____

CHAPTER

10 **VOCABULARY REVIEW WORKSHEET**

Riddle Me This

After completing Chapter 10, give this puzzle a try!

Using each of the clues below, fill in the letters of the word or phrase being described in the blanks provided on the next page. Then read the words in the vertical box to discover the answer to the following riddle: What do you call a feline unhappy about the excessive thermal energy beneath its feet?

1. the reason a spoon gets hot when it is in a bowl of hot soup

2. the conversion of a substance from one physical form to another

3. the energy needed to change the temperature of 1 kg of a substance by 1°C

4. the Earth's atmosphere trapping thermal energy radiated by the sun

5. the transfer of thermal energy by the movement of a liquid or gas

6. the total kinetic energy of the particles in a substance

7. the transfer of energy between objects that are at different temperatures

8. excessive heating of a body of water

9. a material that conducts thermal energy well

10. a machine that uses heat to do work

11. the increase in the volume of a substance due to an increase in temperature

12. the transfer of thermal energy through space

13. the measure of the average kinetic energy of the particles in an object

14. a material that conducts thermal energy poorly

15. the lowest temperature on the Kelvin scale

16. solid, liquid, and gas

Riddle Me This, continued

1. ___ ___ ___ ___ ___ ___ ___ ___ ___

2. ___ ___ ___ ___ ___ ___ ___ ___ ___ ___ ___ ___

3. ___ ___ ___ ___ ___ ___ ___ ___ ___ ___ ___ ___ ___

4. ___ ___ ___ ___ ___ ___ ___ ___ ___ ___ ___ ___

5. ___ ___ ___ ___ ___ ___ ___ ___ ___

6. ___ ___ ___ ___ ___ ___ ___ ___ ___ ___

7. ___ ___ ___ ___

8. ___ ___ ___ ___ ___ ___ ___ ___ ___

9. ___ ___ ___ ___ ___ ___ ___

10. ___ ___ ___ ___ ___ ___ ___ ___

11. ___ ___ ___ ___ ___ ___ ___ ___ ___

12. ___ ___ ___ ___ ___ ___

13. ___ ___ ___ ___ ___ ___ ___ ___

14. ___ ___ ___ ___ ___ ___

15. ___ ___ ___ ___ ___ ___ ___ ___ ___

16. ___ ___ ___ ___ ___ ___ ___ ___ ___

CHAPTER

11 REINFORCEMENT WORKSHEET

Atomic Timeline

Complete this worksheet after you have finished reading Chapter 11, Section 1.
The table below contains a number of statements connected to major discoveries in the development of atomic theory.

1. In each box, write the name of the scientist(s) associated with the statement. Choose from among the following scientists:

- Democritus
- Thomson
- Bohr

- Rutherford
- Dalton
- Schrödinger and Heisenberg

2. On a separate sheet of paper, construct a timeline, and label the following: 440 B.C., 1803, 1897, 1911, 1913, and the twentieth century. Cut out the boxes below along the dotted lines, and tape or glue each box of information at the correct point along your timeline.

There are small, negatively charged particles inside an atom.	Electron paths cannot be predicted.
There is a small, dense, positively charged nucleus.	Electrons travel in definite paths.
Most of an atom's mass is in the nucleus.	Electrons move in empty space in the atom.
Electrons jump between levels from path to path.	His theory of atomic structure led to the "plum-pudding" model.
He conducted the cathode-ray tube experiment.	Electrons are found in electron clouds, not paths.
Atoms of different elements are different.	Atoms of the same element are exactly alike.
Atoms contain mostly empty space.	Atoms constantly move.
Atoms are small, hard particles.	All substances are made of atoms.
He conducted experiments in combining elements.	He conducted the gold foil experiment.
Atoms are "uncuttable."	Elements combine in specific proportions.

CHAPTER

11 VOCABULARY REVIEW WORKSHEET

Atomic Anagrams

Try this anagram after you have finished Chapter 11.
Use the definitions below to unscramble the vocabulary words.

1. weighted average of the masses of all naturally occurring isotopes of the same element

MICTOA SAMS _____

2. the building blocks of matter

MOATS _____

3. unifying scientific explanation supported by testing

RYTHOE _____

4. positively charged particle in the atom

TORPNO _____

5. made up of protons and neutrons

UCSELUN _____

6. particle in the atom that has no charge

TRONUNE _____

7. atoms with the same number of protons but different numbers of neutrons

SOOTPIES _____

8. negatively charged particle in the atom

CLEENROT _____

9. number of protons in a nucleus

MICOTA BRUMEN _____

10. representation of an object or system

OLDEM _____

11. regions where electrons are likely to be found

RENECTOL SCUDLO _____

12. SI unit used to express the mass of atomic particles

MUA _____

13. sum of protons and neutrons

SAMS BRUNEM _____

CHAPTER

12 REINFORCEMENT WORKSHEET

Placing All Your Elements on the Table

Complete this worksheet after you have finished reading Chapter 12, Section 2.

You can tell a lot about the properties of an element just by looking at the element's location on the periodic table. This worksheet will help you better understand the connection between the periodic table and the properties of the elements. Follow the directions below, and use crayons or colored pencils to color the periodic table at the bottom of the page.

1. Color the square for hydrogen yellow.

2. Color the groups with very reactive metals red.

3. Color and label the noble gases orange.

4. Color the transition metals green.

5. Using black, mark the zigzag line that shows the position of the metalloids.

6. Color the metalloids purple.

7. Use blue to color all of the nonmetals that are not noble gases.

8. Color the metals in Groups 13–16 brown.

9. Circle and label the actinides in yellow.

10. Circle and label the lanthanides in red.

11. Circle and label the alkali metals in blue.

12. Circle and label the alkaline-earth metals in purple.

13. Circle and label the halogens in green.

Answer the following questions using the periodic table on the previous page.

14. The alkaline-earth metals react similarly because they all have the same number of electrons in their outer energy level. Which group contains the alkaline-earth metals?

_____

15. How many electrons are in the outer energy level of the

atoms of alkaline-earth metals? _____

16. Hydrogen is in a different color than the rest of the elements in Group 1. Give an example of how hydrogen's characteristics set it apart from other Group 1 elements.

_____

_____

17. What is the name for the group of elements that are particularly unreactive?

_____

18. Except for the metalloids, what do all of the elements on the right side of the zigzag line have in common?

  a. They are not very reactive.   **c.** They are all metals.
  b. They are all nonmetals.   **d.** They are all very reactive.

19. Lanthanide and actinide elements are transition metals.

  True or False? (Circle one.)

Imagine you are a scientist who has just discovered a new element. The element has an atomic number of 113, and it has three electrons in the outer energy level of each atom.

20. Where would you place this new element in the periodic table?

_____

21. Which element would have properties most similar to the new element?

  a. hydrogen   **c.** boron
  b. beryllium   **d.** carbon

22. What name would you suggest for this new element?

_____

CHAPTER
12 **VOCABULARY REVIEW WORKSHEET**

Bringing It to the Periodic Table

Complete the following puzzle after you finish reading Chapter 12.

On the next page is a partially filled-in quotation by Dmitri Mendeleev. Fill in the term described by each clue below. Then put the numbered letters into the corresponding squares on the next page to find out what Mendeleev said. The answers to questions 9–11 are chemical symbols.

1. states that the properties of elements are periodic functions of their atomic numbers

‾‾ ‾‾ ‾‾ ‾‾ ‾‾ ‾‾ ‾‾ ‾‾   ‾‾ ‾‾ ‾‾ ‾‾
59   16   27 40 24   41

2. column or family in the periodic table

‾‾ ‾‾ ‾‾ ‾‾ ‾‾ ‾‾
19 35 58

3. any element in Groups 3–12

‾‾ ‾‾ ‾‾ ‾‾ ‾‾ ‾‾ ‾‾ ‾‾ ‾‾ ‾‾ ‾‾ ‾‾
31   14   43   55 18   7 33 10

4. elements in Group 1

‾‾ ‾‾ ‾‾ ‾‾ ‾‾ ‾‾ ‾‾ ‾‾ ‾‾ ‾‾ ‾‾
17   22   48   8   36   11

5. having a regular, repeating pattern

‾‾ ‾‾ ‾‾ ‾‾ ‾‾ ‾‾ ‾‾ ‾‾
52   15   25   28 23

6. metals with two electrons in the outer energy level

‾‾ ‾‾ ‾‾ ‾‾ ‾‾ ‾‾ ‾ ‾‾ ‾‾ ‾‾ ‾‾
51   50   20   42   54   2

7. a row of elements

‾‾ ‾‾ ‾‾ ‾‾ ‾‾ ‾‾
61 6 26   56

8. elements that don't react readily with other elements

‾‾ ‾‾ ‾‾ ‾‾ ‾‾ ‾‾ ‾‾ ‾‾ ‾‾ ‾‾
29   49   62   44   64

9. atomic number 9

‾‾ ‾‾
13

10. atomic number 39

‾‾ ‾‾
57

11. atomic number 54

‾‾ ‾‾
47 63

Bringing It to the Periodic Table, continued

12. elements having properties of metals and nonmetals

—— —— —— —— —— —— —— —— —— ——
39 46 37   5   12

13. the first row of transition metals at the bottom of the periodic table

—— —— —— —— —— —— —— —— —— —— ——
        1   9   34   4

14. the most abundant element in the universe

—— —— —— —— —— —— —— ——
        21   38   3

15. group containing iodine and chlorine

—— —— —— —— —— —— —— ——
32   60 30 53   45

Mendeleev's Quotation:

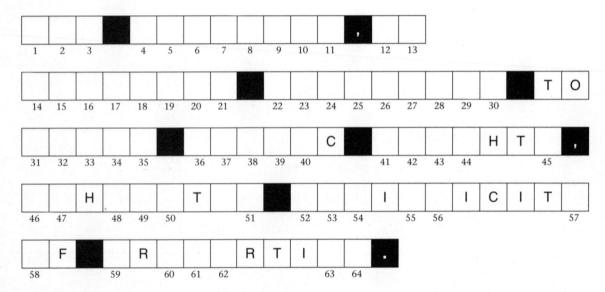

Is It an Ion?

Complete this worksheet after you finish reading Chapter 13, Section 2.

Answer the following questions based on the accompanying models. Protons are shown in gray, neutrons are shown in white, and electrons are shown in black.

Answer Questions 1–6 based on Figure 1.

1. How many protons are shown? _____

2. In the periodic table, elements are ordered by atomic number, the number of protons in an atom's nucleus. Using the periodic table in your textbook, identify the element shown.

   _____

3. How many electrons are shown? _____

4. How many electrons are in the outermost energy

   level? _____

Figure 1

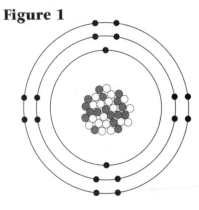

5. If the number of electrons equals the number of protons, then there is no charge, and the model shows a neutral atom. If the numbers are not equal, then you have an ion. Use this reasoning to determine if Figure 1 shows an ion or a neutral atom.

   _____

6. To determine a particle's charge, you must compare the number of protons with the number of electrons. Use the spaces to the right to subtract the number of electrons from the number of protons. (Remember, if the number of electrons is greater than the number of protons, the charge will be negative.)

Number of protons	_____
Number of electrons	− _____
Charge of model	_____

Answer Questions 7–11 based on Figure 2.

7. How many protons are shown? _____

8. What element is it? _____

9. How many electrons are shown? _____

10. How many electrons are in the outermost energy

    level? _____

11. Is this an ion? If it is, calculate and record the charge.

    _____

    _____

    _____

Figure 2

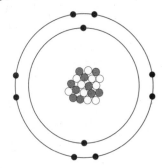

Interview with an Electron

Complete this worksheet after you finish reading Chapter 13, Section 2.

The following descriptions are from the point of view of electrons that are participating in three different types of bonds—ionic, metallic, and covalent. Identify the type of bond that each electron describes. At the bottom of the page is a list of characteristics of bonds and substances containing the bonds. Match each characteristic with the corresponding bond, and write the characteristic in the space provided.

1. My buddies and I do not feel bound to the energy level of one atom in particular, so we can swim freely throughout the substance.

Type of bond: _____

Characteristics: _____

_____

_____

2. I might change sides at the start, but once I end up on one side or the other I stick to my decision.

Type of bond: _____

Characteristics: _____

_____

3. I do not feel partial to either of the atoms in my bond. To be fair, the other bonding electron and I divide our time between the bonded atoms.

Type of bond: _____

Characteristics: _____

_____

_____

Characteristics

- Compounds have a crystal-lattice structure.

- Substances are good conductors of electric current.

- There's an attraction between nuclei and shared electrons.

- There's a transfer of electrons.

- Two or more nonmetals are involved.

- There's an attraction of positive ions and free-moving electrons.

- A metal reacts with a nonmetal.

CHAPTER
13 **VOCABULARY REVIEW WORKSHEET**

Bonding Puzzle

After completing Chapter 13, give this puzzle a try!

Fill in the blanks in the clues below. Then use the clues to complete the puzzle on the next page.

Clues

1. An arrangement of ions bonded in a repeating three-dimensional pattern is a _____ .

2. A positive particle in the nucleus that attracts electrons is a _____ .

3. A unifying explanation for a broad range of hypotheses and observations that have been supported by testing is called a

_____ .

4. The force of attraction that holds two atoms together is called a(n) _____ .

5. An electron in the outermost energy level of an atom is called a

_____ .

6. The force of attraction between oppositely charged ions is a(n)

_____ .

7. The _____ is a chart that displays all elements by atomic number, and can be used to determine the number of valence electrons for some elements.

8. A _____ is an element composed of molecules consisting of two atoms of that element.

9. The joining of atoms to form new substances is called

_____ .

10. The force of attraction between the nuclei of atoms and the

shared electrons is called a(n) _____ .

11. A _____ is a neutral group of atoms held together by covalent bonds.

12. The force of attraction between a positively charged metal ion and the electrons in a metal is called a(n)

_____ .

13. A(n) _____ is a charged particle that forms when one or more valence electrons are transferred from one atom to another.

P	T	E	A	R	B	I	L	O	E	O	M	I	D	C	I	A
T	C	H	E	M	I	C	A	L	B	O	N	D	I	N	G	T
O	N	R	Y	B	O	N	T	M	L	I	C	E	D	N	O	I
L	O	E	Y	E	C	M	E	E	N	T	C	H	N	E	M	I
C	R	A	M	S	B	L	C	B	O	I	N	D	O	N	D	G
M	T	T	E	E	T	U	A	I	O	N	I	C	B	O	N	D
C	C	R	T	Y	L	A	S	T	A	L	L	C	L	M	O	L
E	E	C	A	E	N	E	L	L	A	V	L	I	A	O	B	L
P	L	R	L	O	C	T	C	L	N	N	T	H	C	E	T	O
R	E	Y	L	O	C	H	E	I	A	O	T	Y	I	A	N	M
I	E	C	I	O	C	B	O	N	M	T	R	C	M	A	E	L
B	C	I	C	O	N	D	V	P	R	O	T	I	E	N	L	B
D	N	O	B	M	E	T	A	L	E	R	T	I	H	C	A	E
M	E	T	O	L	I	C	I	H	A	P	L	A	C	E	V	N
E	L	E	N	E	N	M	T	C	E	E	L	E	I	E	O	C
T	A	R	D	O	N	S	I	B	O	O	N	D	I	D	C	C
M	V	O	L	E	L	B	A	T	C	I	D	O	I	R	E	P

Name _____ Date _____ Class _____

Fabulous Food Reactions

Complete this worksheet after you finish reading Chapter 14, Section 2.

In your textbook, you read how dancers can model different chemical reactions. Another way to model chemical reactions is to use food. In the spaces provided, write the type of chemical reaction that is modeled in situations 1–4 below. The possible chemical reactions are *synthesis, decomposition, single-replacement,* and *double-replacement.* Then answer question 5.

1. One day, Oriana packed a ham-on-wheat sandwich, and her friend, Macha, packed a salami-on-rye sandwich. At lunch, they decided to trade meats. Oriana ate a salami-on-wheat sandwich, while Macha ate a ham-on-rye sandwich.

_____

2. Yasu went to an Italian restaurant. When asked for his order he said, "I'd like the Pasta Extravaganza, but could I have meatball sauce instead of the alfredo sauce?"

_____

3. Tara ordered a side order of mixed vegetables with her meal. But before eating them, she separated the vegetables into separate portions of peas and carrots.

_____

4. Kevin went to a salad bar. He used lettuce and tomatoes to make his salad.

_____

5. Hydrogen and oxygen combine to form water. How is this similar to one of the situations given above?

_____

_____

_____

_____

_____

_____

CHAPTER

14 **REINFORCEMENT WORKSHEET**

Activation Energy

Complete this worksheet after you finish reading Chapter 14, Section 3.

Activation energy is the energy a reaction needs to get started. At the bottom of the page are two energy diagrams—one for an exothermic reaction and one for an endothermic reaction. Follow the directions below to label the energy diagrams.

1. In an exothermic reaction, the chemical energy of the reactants is greater than the chemical energy of the products. Write *Exothermic reaction* under the appropriate energy diagram.

2. In an endothermic reaction, the chemical energy of the reactants is lower than the chemical energy of the products. Write *Endothermic reaction* under the appropriate energy diagram.

3. Exothermic reactions give off energy. The energy given off is the difference between the energy of the reactants and the energy of the products. Label the energy given off on the exothermic-energy diagram by writing *Energy given off* in the appropriate space.

4. Endothermic reactions absorb energy. The energy absorbed by a chemical reaction is the difference between the energy of the products and the energy of the reactants. Label the energy absorbed on the endothermic energy diagram by writing *Energy absorbed* in the appropriate space.

5. The activation energy is the energy needed to start a chemical reaction. On the diagrams below, the chemical reaction begins at the top of the peak. The activation energy is the difference between the top of the peak and the energy of the reactants. Label the activation energy of each graph by writing *Activation energy* in the appropriate space.

Energy Diagrams for an Endothermic and an Exothermic Reaction

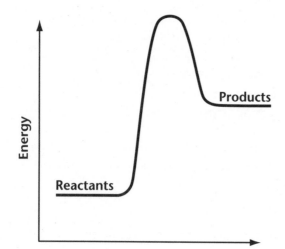

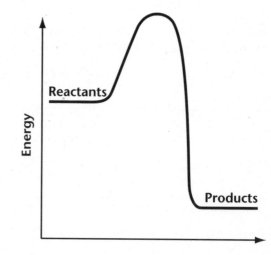

A Reactionary Puzzle

After reading Chapter 14, give this puzzle a try!

Fill in the blanks in the clues below. Then use the clues to complete the puzzle on the next page.

1. A number written below and to the right of a chemical symbol in a formula is called a _____ .

2. In a _____ -replacement reaction, ions in two compounds switch places.

3. The _____ energy is the minimum amount of energy required for substances to react.

4. A chemical _____ is the process by which one or more substances undergo change to produce one or more different substances.

5. The law of _____ of _____ states that mass cannot be created or destroyed in ordinary chemical or physical changes. A similar law holds true for _____ .

6. In a _____ reaction, a single compound breaks down to form two or more simpler substances.

7. In _____ reactions energy is released, and in _____ reactions energy is absorbed.

8. In a _____ reaction, two or more substances combine to form a single compound.

9. A chemical _____ describes a substance using chemical symbols and numbers.

10. A number written to the left of a chemical symbol or formula is called a _____ .

11. In a _____ -replacement reaction, one element replaces another that is part of a compound.

12. A chemical _____ is a shorthand description of a chemical reaction.

13. In a chemical reaction, each starting material is a _____ , and each new substance formed is a _____ .

14. A _____ speeds up a reaction, and an _____ slows down a reaction.

A Reactionary Puzzle, continued

How many chapter concepts can you find in the block of letters below? Use the clues to help you find them. Words may appear horizontally, vertically, or diagonally.

D	C	Q	R	E	A	C	T	A	N	T	B	Y	C
C	E	X	O	T	H	E	R	M	I	C	G	A	O
D	O	C	A	T	A	L	Y	S	T	R	E	K	E
S	T	N	O	R	V	P	I	I	E	J	I	A	F
U	F	V	S	M	N	S	I	N	G	L	E	C	F
B	O	U	Y	E	P	X	E	H	J	E	R	T	I
S	R	F	N	Q	R	O	Q	I	Q	Q	E	I	C
C	M	J	T	T	O	V	S	B	Z	U	A	V	I
R	U	O	H	O	D	M	A	I	P	A	C	A	E
I	L	R	E	S	U	F	G	T	T	T	T	T	N
P	A	I	S	A	C	I	F	O	I	I	I	I	T
T	U	A	I	K	T	A	U	R	D	O	O	O	G
F	M	H	S	D	O	U	B	L	E	N	N	N	D
E	N	D	O	T	H	E	R	M	I	C	Q	N	K

A Simple Solution

Complete this worksheet after you finish reading Chapter 15, Section 2.

Libby Lidmis has been busy gathering information on acids, bases, and salts. Unfortunately, someone mixed up the information on her chart. Each of the pieces of information given below describes an acid, a base, or a salt. Help Libby straighten out her chart by matching each piece of information with the correct categories, and writing it in the appropriate box on the next page. Be careful—some of the pieces of information belong in more than one category.

- taste bitter

- may be corrosive

- used to de-ice roads

- excess hydroxide ions

- found in drain cleaner

- found in plasterboard

- react with baking soda to produce carbon dioxide gas

- change blue litmus to red

- pH less than 7

- used to make soap

- H^+

- form from a neutralization reaction

- change red litmus to blue

- sodium chloride

- found in vinegar

- taste sour

- neutralize lakes with low pH

- OH^-

- excess hydronium ions

- pH greater than 7

- slippery

- found in orange juice

- form from the reaction of a metal and a nonmetal

ACIDS

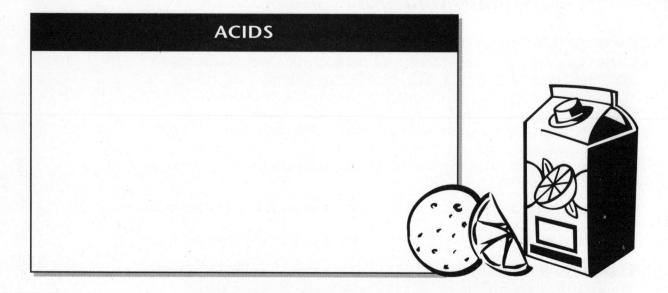

BASES

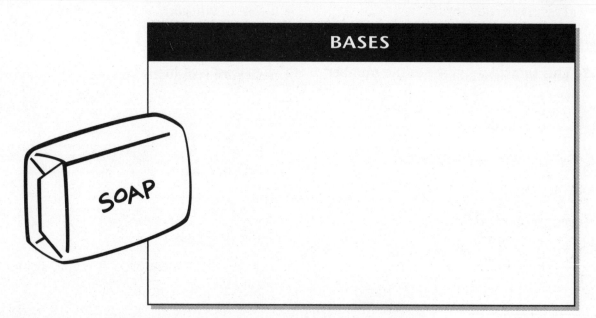

SALTS

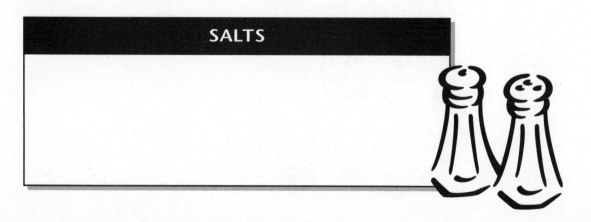

CHAPTER

15 VOCABULARY REVIEW WORKSHEET

Compounding the Problem

Use the clues below and on the next page to identify vocabulary terms from Chapter 15. Then find and circle each term in the word search puzzle on the next page.

1. Many fuels are made of these organic compounds.

_____

2. Atoms share electrons in _____ compounds.

3. _____ are sometimes called the "blue-prints of life."

4. The measure of the concentration of hydronium ions in a solution is known as _____ .

5. Plants tend to store these as oils. _____

6. The positive ion of a base and the negative ion of an acid combine to form this ionic compound. _____

7. This substance increases the number of H⁺ when dissolved in water. _____

8. _____ are organic compounds made by living things.

9. This substance is slippery and bitter. _____

10. These biochemicals are composed of one or more simple sugar molecules bonded together. _____

11. These compounds contain oppositely charged ions arranged in a crystal lattice. _____

12. These compounds are composed of molecules whose carbon atoms are arranged in a straight chain, a branched chain, or a ring

_____

13. _____ are biochemicals that have many functions, such as regulating chemical activities.

14. This special paper is used to test for acids and bases.

_____

15. The building blocks of proteins are _____ .

16. This protein regulates the amount of glucose in your blood.

_____

Compounding the Problem, continued

---

17. This type of carbohydrate, found in bread, cereal, and pasta, is called a _____ carbohydrate.

18. This substance changes color in the presence of an acid or a base.

_____

19. A carbon atom can form no more than this number of bonds.

_____

20. This type of nucleic acid is the genetic material of the cell.

_____

21. This type of hydrocarbon contains carbon atoms connected only by single bonds. _____

22. _____ is a protein that carries oxygen to all parts of your body.

Y	X	B	H	T	A	R	O	T	A	C	I	D	N	I	A
J	C	E	I	P	N	X	A	B	R	M	W	S	O	N	L
A	H	I	L	O	T	E	I	O	B	I	A	E	D	I	T
S	W	L	N	P	C	L	P	D	I	L	S	C	P	I	L
N	S	R	A	A	M	H	A	K	X	A	A	I	N	Y	N
O	D	S	C	G	G	O	E	S	B	R	D	I	D	C	I
B	I	N	K	A	A	R	C	M	B	S	L	M	V	H	B
R	C	I	Z	V	U	U	O	O	I	U	W	N	U	P	O
A	A	E	J	O	E	Y	H	C	S	C	Q	P	H	G	L
C	O	T	F	A	E	Y	O	N	A	L	A	E	T	X	G
O	N	O	V	W	D	V	I	H	H	C	I	L	I	G	O
R	I	R	L	R	A	I	X	Y	F	M	I	T	S	Q	M
D	M	P	A	L	O	J	K	V	K	K	T	D	M	H	E
Y	A	T	E	N	G	L	V	P	B	E	D	U	Q	U	H
H	E	N	I	N	B	D	E	T	A	R	U	T	A	S	S
S	T	C	N	U	C	L	E	I	C	A	C	I	D	S	R

CHAPTER
16 REINFORCEMENT WORKSHEET

The Decay of a Nucleus

Complete this worksheet after you finish reading Chapter 16, Section 1.

Fill in the blanks in items 1–4, and then complete the table at the bottom of the page.

1. An alpha particle is the same as the nucleus of an atom of the element

_____ . It contains _____ neutron(s)

and _____ proton(s).

2. During alpha decay, the atomic number decreases by _____

and the mass number _____ by four.

3. In one type of beta decay, a neutron in a radioactive nucleus breaks down into a

_____ and a(n) _____ .

4. When a radioactive nucleus releases a beta particle, its atomic number increases by

one, and the mass number _____ .
(decreases, stays the same, or increases)

In the text, you learned that a uranium-238 nucleus undergoes 14 decays to become lead-206. Now you can construct a decay series by completing the table below. You will need the periodic table of the elements. The first two steps have been done for you. (Hint: All beta particles released in this series are electrons, not positrons.)

Step	Type of decay	New atomic number	New mass number	Name of isotope formed
		92	238	U-238
1	Alpha	90	234	Th-234
2	Beta	91	234	Pa-234
3	Beta			
4	Alpha			
5	Alpha			
6	Alpha			
7	Alpha			
8	Alpha			
9	Beta			
10	Beta			
11	Alpha			
12	Beta			
13	Beta			
14	Alpha			

Fission or Fusion?

Complete this worksheet after you finish reading Chapter 16, Section 2.

While it's true that fusion and fission are both types of nuclear reactions, the similarity ends there. Follow the steps below to sort out the facts and eliminate any con-*fusion*!

1. Take a look at the illustrations in the table below. In the first column, label each illustration either "fusion" or "fission."

2. Read over the following list of information. Then write each piece of information next to the appropriate type of nuclear reaction. Answers may be used more than once.

- Chernobyl
- not currently used to provide electrical energy
- hydrogen is a plasma
- fuels 20 percent of the electrical energy used in the United States
- requires temperatures over 100,000,000°C
- radioactive waste products

- occurs in the sun's core
- no radioactive waste products
- energy is released
- large nucleus splits into two smaller nuclei
- uranium
- two or more nuclei join together to form a more-massive nucleus

Nuclear Reaction Chart	
_____	
_____	

CHAPTER

16 VOCABULARY REVIEW WORKSHEET

Atomic Energy Acrostic

After you finish Chapter 16, give this puzzle a try!

Fill in the blanks below. Then put letters into the matching numbered squares to reveal a quote by Marie Curie.

1. occurs when two or more small nuclei join together to form a larger, more-massive nucleus

___ ___ ___ ___ ___ ___ ___ ___ ___ ___
             20 38   9

2. decay that occurs when a nucleus releases a positron or an electron

___ ___ ___ ___ ___
     13

3. the ability of the nuclei of some atoms to give off high-energy particles and rays

___ ___ ___ ___ ___ ___ ___ ___ ___ ___ ___
23   8 45   5   27

4. the collective name of high-energy particles and rays given off by the nuclei of atoms

___ ___ ___ ___ ___ ___ ___ ___ ___ ___ ___ ___ ___
                  42   40   3   30

5. the process by which high-energy particles and rays are released

___ ___ ___ ___ ___ ___ ___ ___ ___ ___ ___ ___ ___
     25   46   34   19   47 37   33

6. atoms with the same number of protons but different numbers of neutrons

___ ___ ___ ___ ___ ___ ___ ___
     15 2 16   41

7. occurs when a large nucleus splits, releasing energy and two smaller nuclei

___ ___ ___ ___ ___ ___ ___ ___   ___ ___ ___ ___ ___ ___
                          11   43   35 6

8. the sum of protons and neutrons in an atom

___ ___ ___ ___ ___ ___ ___
     22   29   1   36

9. high-energy light waves that are released from a radioactive nucleus during alpha decay and beta decay

___ ___ ___ ___ ___ ___   ___ ___ ___ ___
7

10. the length of time it takes for one-half of the nuclei of a
radioactive isotope to decay

— — —̲ — —   — —̲ —̲ —̲
      32   28 12 24

11. occurs when a nucleus releases a particle consisting of two
protons and two neutrons

— —̲ — —̲ —   — — — — —
    10   4

12. the isotope often used to determine the age of once-living things

— — — —̲ —̲ —̲-14
          18 17

13. a continuous series of nuclear fission reactions

— — — — — — —   — — — —̲ —̲
                                    26 39

—̲ — — —̲ —̲ — —̲
21   44 14   31

What Marie Curie said:

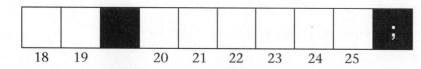

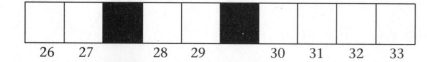

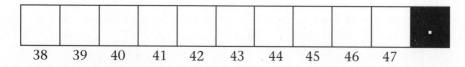

CHAPTER

17 **REINFORCEMENT WORKSHEET**

Charge!

Complete this worksheet after you have finished reading Chapter 17, Section 1.

There are three ways for an object to gain a charge: friction, conduction, and induction. When it loses its charge it experiences electric discharge. Label the following pictures as examples of *conduction, induction, friction,* or *electric discharge.*

1.

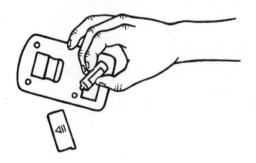

_____

2.

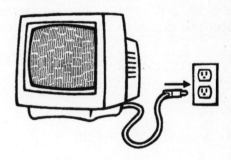

_____

3.

_____

4.

_____

5.

_____

6.

_____

CHAPTER

17 **REINFORCEMENT WORKSHEET**

Electric Circuits

Complete this worksheet after you have finished reading Chapter 17, Section 4.

Two electric circuits powered by cells are shown below. Answer the following questions based on the information given in the diagrams. Questions 1–6 refer to Figure 1, and Questions 8–12 refer to Figure 2.

Label the parts of the circuit and the cell by writing the letter that corresponds to the appropriate part in the space provided.

1. _____ load

2. _____ electrode

3. _____ wire

4. _____ electrolyte

5. _____ energy source

6. Is this circuit connected in series or in parallel?

_____

Figure 1

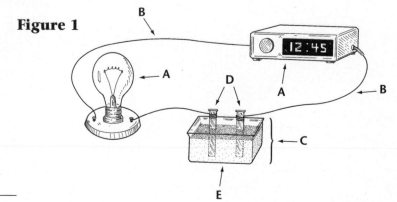

7. A cell that contains liquid electrolytes is called a _____ cell.

Figure 2

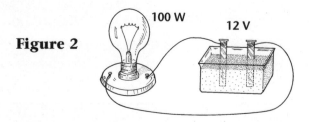

8. What is the power in this circuit? _____

9. What is the voltage in this circuit? _____

10. Recall that $I = P/V$. If you divide the power of the circuit by its voltage, you'll get the circuit's current. What is the current of this circuit?

_____

11. Remember that Ohm's law can be rearranged to say: $R = V/I$. If you divide the circuit's voltage by its current, you'll get the resistance of the circuit. What is the resistance caused by the light bulb?

_____

12. This cell contains a solid electrolyte, so it is a _____ cell.

An Electrifying Puzzle

Now that you have read Chapter 17, give this crossword puzzle a try!

ACROSS

3. type of circuit in which different loads are on separate branches

4. a material in which charges cannot easily move

5. the rate at which charge passes a given point

6. The energy per unit charge is called the _____ difference.

7. The law of electric _____ s states that like charges repel and opposite charges attract.

11. a device in a circuit that uses electrical energy to do work

15. converts thermal energy into electrical energy

17. consists of several cells

18. a complete, closed path through which electric charges flow

19. the opposition to the flow of electric charge

20. used to open and close a circuit

DOWN

1. a device that produces an electric current by converting chemical energy into electrical energy

2. Electric _____ is the loss of static electricity as charges move off an object.

3. the part of a solar panel that absorbs light and converts it into electrical energy

5. transfer of electrons from one object to another by direct contact

8. rearrangement of electrons on an uncharged object without direct contact with a charged object

9. A charged object exerts an electric _____ on other charged objects.

10. Electric _____ is the rate at which electrical energy does work.

12. a material in which charges can move easily

13. The buildup of electric charges on an object is called _____ electricity.

14. the difference in energy per unit charge as a charge moves between two points in the path of a circuit

16. type of circuit in which all parts are connected in a single loop

An Electrifying Puzzle, continued

Planet Lodestone

Complete this worksheet after reading Chapter 18, Section 1.

After months in space, Captain Iva Braveheart and her crew are approaching their destination—the planet Lodestone. Read the following entries in Captain Braveheart's personal spacelog, and answer the questions.

Earth date July 21, 2313

Finally, we are drawing near to the planet Lodestone. Tomorrow we should be close enough to perform some tests on the planet. I am most curious to know what the planet's core is like—and whether compasses are likely to work on this planet.

1. What properties of planet Lodestone's core would indicate that the planet probably has magnetic properties?

_____

_____

_____

Earth date July 22, 2313

Our tests indicate that the planet should have magnetic poles, just like Earth. A small team will visit the planet's surface tomorrow. I'm going to take along a bar magnet and string to find magnetic north and south on Lodestone.

2. How will the captain find magnetic north and south on this planet using a bar magnet and string?

_____

_____

_____

_____

3. Captain Braveheart plans to name geographic North on planet Lodestone after magnetic north and geographic South after magnetic south. If she does, will North and South be the same on Lodestone as they are on Earth? Explain.

_____

_____

_____

18 REINFORCEMENT WORKSHEET

A Magnetic Time

Complete this worksheet after reading Chapter 18, Section 3.

1. Draw a line from the person or group of people in Column A to their contribution to the study of electromagnetism in Column B. Be careful; two scientists match with one contribution.

2. Draw a line from the contribution in Column B to the year or time period when it occurred in Column C.

Column A	Column B	Column C
Hans Christian Oersted	proposed that the Earth is one giant magnet	2,000 years ago
Michael Faraday	found a mineral called magnetite, which attracts iron-containing objects	1831
Greeks	found that a changing magnetic field could induce an electric current	1600
William Gilbert	after many experiments, concluded that an electric current produces a magnetic field	1820
Joseph Henry		

3. Use the information above to create a timeline in the space below.

CHAPTER

18   VOCABULARY REVIEW WORKSHEET

A Puzzling Transformation

After you finish Chapter 18, try this puzzle!

Using each of the clues below, fill in the letters of the word or phrase being described on the blanks provided on the next page.

1. Force between two magnets

2. Parts of a magnet where the magnetic effects are strongest

3. Device used to measure current

4. Device that changes electrical energy into kinetic energy

5. Produced by a coil of current-carrying wire wrapped around an iron core

6. Scientist who discovered the relationship between electricity and magnetism

7. During electromagnetic _____, a changing magnetic field produces an electric current.

8. Magnet made with iron, nickel, or cobalt

9. British scientist who discovered that a changing magnetic field can produce an electric current

10. Abbreviation for magnetic levitation

11. A tiny region in a magnet where all the atoms are grouped together and their poles are aligned

12. Region around a magnet in which magnetic force can act

13. Device that uses electromagnetic induction to convert kinetic energy into electrical energy

14. Coil of wire that, when carrying an electric current, produces a magnetic field

15. Device that increases or decreases the voltage of an alternating current

16. Material that attracts iron or materials containing iron

A Puzzling Transformation, *continued*

1. __ __ __ __ **E** __ __ __   __ __ __ __ __

2. __ __ **L** __ __

3. __ __ __ __ __ __ __ __ **E** __ __ __

4. __ __ __ __ __ __ **C** __ __ __ __

5. __ __ __ __ **T** __ __ __ __ __

6. __ __ **R** __ __ __ __ __

7. __ __ __ __ __ __ **O** __

8. __ __ __ __ __ **M** __ __ __ __

9. __ **A** __ __ __ __ __

10. __ __ **G** __ __ __

11. __ __ __ __ **N** __

12. __ __ __ __ **E** __ __ __   __ __ __ __

13. __ __ __ __ __ __ **T** __ __

14. __ __ __ __ __ __ __ **I** __

15. __ __ __ __ **S** __ __ __ __ __

16. **M** __ __ __ __ __

CHAPTER

19 **REINFORCEMENT WORKSHEET**

Semiconductors' Conductivity

Complete this worksheet after reading Chapter 19, Section 1.

A semiconductor is a material that conducts electrical energy better than an insulator but not as well as a conductor. Silicon may be the most well-known semiconductor, but it's not the only one. Another semiconductor is germanium (Ge). Use the periodic table in your textbook to help you answer the following questions.

1. Like silicon, germanium has _____ electrons in the outermost energy level of each atom.

Doping a semiconductor means replacing a few atoms of the semiconductor with a few atoms of another substance that has a different number of valence electrons.

2. Germanium can be doped with antimony (Sb), a group _____

element, which has _____ electrons in the outermost energy level of each atom.

3. Germanium can be doped with indium (In), a group _____

element, which has _____ electrons in the outermost energy level of each atom.

4. In the space below, sketch the arrangement of electrons in pure germanium, in germanium doped with antimony, and in germanium doped with indium. Draw only the electrons in the outermost energy levels. The outermost energy level of each atom is represented by a gray circle.

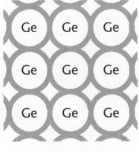

germanium

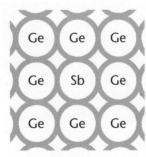

germanium-
antimony

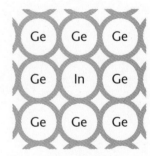

germanium-
indium

An n-type semiconductor is a doped semiconductor with an "extra" electron. A p-type semiconductor is a doped semiconductor with a "hole" where an electron could be.

5. Doping germanium with _____ results in an n-type semiconductor.

6. Doping germanium with _____ results in a p-type semiconductor.

CHAPTER
19 **REINFORCEMENT WORKSHEET**

The Ins and Outs of Computing

Complete this worksheet after you finish Chapter 19, Section 3.

Fill in the blanks in the paragraph below with the terms *input device,
microprocessor, memory,* and *output device.*

1. Information is entered into a computer using a(n)

_____ . The information is processed by the

central processing unit, which is a(n) _____ ,

or the information is stored in the computer's

_____ until it is needed. When a computer

finishes a task, it shows the results on a(n)

_____ .

2. Below is an illustration of a desktop computer setup. Label the
parts of the computer with the following terms: *speaker, monitor,
keyboard, mouse, floppy disk, printer.*

3. Using colored pencils or crayons, color input devices yellow,
output devices red, and storage and processing devices blue.

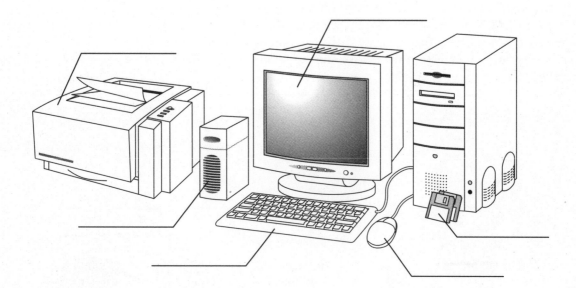

4. The computer shown above does not have a modem. If it did,
what color would you shade the modem? Explain.

_____

_____

_____

CHAPTER

19 VOCABULARY REVIEW WORKSHEET

A Circuit-ous Crossword

After you finish Chapter 19, try this crossword puzzle!

ACROSS

1. something that represents information

2. a huge computer network consisting of millions of computers that can share information with each other

6. an entire circuit formed on a single silicon chip

13. conducts electric current better than an insulator but not as well as a conductor

14. an electronic device that performs tasks by processing and storing information

15. integrated circuit that contains many of a computer's capabilities on a single chip

16. _____ tubes can perform the same functions as transistors, but they are larger, give off more thermal energy, and don't last as long.

DOWN

1. set of instructions or commands that tells a computer what to do

3. type of wave that consists of changing electric and magnetic waves

4. an electronic component that allows current in only one direction

5. a collection of tiny circuits that supply electric current to the parts of an electronic device

7. type of signal whose properties can change continuously according to changes in the original information

8. type of signal that consists of a series of electric pulses represented by the digits of binary numbers

9. an electronic component composed of three layers of semiconductors

10. the sending of information across long distances by electronic means

11. the parts or equipment that make up a computer

12. process that modifies the conductivity of a semiconductor

A Circuit-ous Crossword, continued

CHAPTER
20 **REINFORCEMENT WORKSHEET**

Getting on the Same Frequency

Complete this worksheet after you finish reading Chapter 20, Section 2.

Examine the diagram below, and then answer the questions that follow.

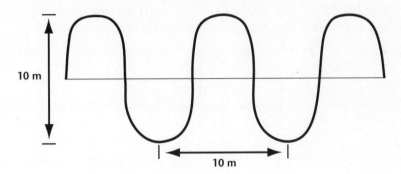

1. What is the amplitude of the wave?

   _____

2. What is the wavelength?

   _____

Remember, frequency, expressed in hertz (Hz), is the number of waves produced in a given amount of time.

3. If you were watching this wave go by and counted five crests passing a certain point in 5 seconds, what would be the frequency of the wave? Use the formula and the space below to calculate your answer.

$$\text{Frequency} = \frac{\text{number of waves}}{\text{time}} =$$

4. What would the frequency of the wave be if you counted 10 crests in five seconds? Use the space below to calculate the answer.

5. If the wavelength became 12 m but the wave speed remained the same, would the frequency increase, decrease, or stay the same?

   _____

CHAPTER
20 **REINFORCEMENT WORKSHEET**

Makin' Waves

Complete this worksheet after you finish reading Chapter 20, Section 3.

Diagram and label the interaction described below, and then answer the questions that follow.

Wave A, with an amplitude of 3 m, meets wave B, with an amplitude of 3 m. When A and B overlap, the wave produced (C) has an amplitude of 6 m.

1. What type of wave interaction is described? Explain.

_____

_____

_____

_____

_____

2. If wave A were to overlap with a different wave to produce a new wave that had an amplitude of 0 m instead of 6 m, would this be the same type of interaction described above? Explain.

_____

_____

_____

_____

_____

CHAPTER

20 VOCABULARY REVIEW WORKSHEET

Let's Do the Wave!

After you finish Chapter 20, give this puzzle a try!

Figure out the words described by the clues below, and write each word in the appropriate space. Then find and circle the words in the puzzle on the next page.

1. _____ a substance through which a wave can travel

2. _____ the bending of a wave as it passes at an angle from one medium to another

3. _____ a disturbance that transmits energy through matter and space

4. _____ when one vibrating object causes similar vibrations in another object that is nearby

5. _____ the lowest point of a transverse wave

6. _____ the number of waves produced in a given amount of time

7. _____ when two or more waves overlap

8. _____ describes lines that meet at right angles

9. _____ an echo, for example (wave interaction)

10. _____ a wave that occurs at the boundary between two media when transverse and longitudinal waves combine

11. _____ wave in which particles in the medium vibrate back and forth along the path the wave travels

12. _____ waves in which particles of the medium vibrate in an up-and-down motion

13. _____ the distance between two adjacent compressions

14. _____ the maximum distance a wave vibrates from its rest position

15. _____ kind of wave that looks like it is stationary

16. _____ the highest point of a transverse wave

17. _____ measurement equal to one wave per second

18. _____ the bending of waves around a barrier or through an opening

Let's Do the Wave! continued

In the puzzle below, find the words from the blanks on the previous page. Words may appear horizontally, vertically, or diagonally.

S	W	V	O	M	Y	O	Y	S	F	S	U	M	V	J	Z	X
U	B	H	C	P	I	C	E	X	T	S	V	G	T	G	C	R
R	A	L	U	C	I	D	N	E	P	R	E	P	M	N	Z	C
F	G	O	V	W	D	S	R	E	F	L	E	C	T	I	O	N
A	T	N	T	R	W	O	L	F	U	L	O	O	K	D	A	T
C	R	G	E	E	N	O	E	W	M	Q	O	M	I	N	M	L
E	A	I	A	F	R	N	S	I	N	G	E	R	A	A	B	O
I	N	T	E	R	F	E	R	E	N	C	E	R	U	T	T	W
W	S	U	V	A	E	S	E	P	R	S	E	T	F	S	T	A
Y	V	D	O	C	O	L	B	N	O	O	U	L	D	N	M	V
T	E	I	O	T	U	S	N	N	A	Y	A	I	C	P	E	E
T	R	N	O	I	T	C	A	R	F	F	I	D	L	M	D	L
R	S	A	M	O	I	N	R	Y	O	E	L	I	P	N	I	E
O	E	L	J	N	C	A	T	N	D	W	T	O	W	H	U	N
U	E	F	H	E	R	T	Z	L	E	U	R	V	E	B	M	G
G	G	I	L	F	U	N	S	L	D	O	U	C	R	E	S	T
H	C	O	D	I	W	A	V	E	A	T	I	Q	U	O	R	H

Doppler Dan's Dump Truck

Complete this worksheet after you finish reading Chapter 21, Section 2.

Doppler Dan the Garbage Man is moving a truckload of glass from one end of the recycling plant to the other. Elinor has just helped him load up all of the broken bottles at the front of the plant on the east side of the lot. As Dan drives away, he honks his horn in thanks to Elinor. He speeds off in a hurry, because his buddy Otis is waiting impatiently on the west side to help him unload the glass from the dump truck.

"Howdy Otis," says Dan, as he drives up.

"Hey," grumbles Otis, chewing on his pen. "Your horn sounds funny."

"Sounds fine to me," says Dan as cheerfully as possible. He thought Otis was just making trouble, as he is not a morning person. Still it seemed like a strange thing to say. Why would the horn sound different to Otis than it did to him?

At the end of the day, Dan was still wondering about Otis's mysterious comment. He decided to ask Elinor about it.

Elinor reminded Dan that he honked the horn as he drove away from her. Then she drew him the diagram below. Points 0–3 represent Dan's positions as he drove from east to west. The compressions of the sound waves made by the honking horn are shown as circles A–D. A is the compression that came from the horn when Dan was at Point 0, B is from Point 1, C is from Point 2, and D is from Point 3.

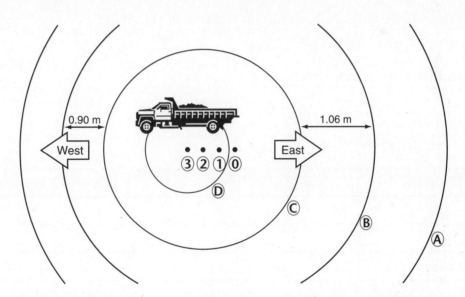

Next Elinor told Dan that by studying the diagram and doing some minor calculations, he could find out the answer. On the next page, follow the steps Dan used to find out why the horn sounded different to Otis. The formulas below will help you.

Formulas	
For the speed of a wave:	wave speed = wavelength × frequency
For wavelength:	wavelength = wave speed ÷ frequency
For frequency:	frequency = wave speed ÷ wavelength

Doppler Dan's Dump Truck, continued

1. Use your textbook to find the speed of sound in air at 20°C.

wave speed = _____

2. Doppler Dan bought his horn from
Honk, Inc. They guaranteed that the
horn will honk at a frequency of 350 Hz.
Use the equation on the previous page to
calculate the wavelength of sound made
by Dan's horn and show your work here.

_____

3. Find the wavelength of the sound by
measuring the distance from one compression to the next. From where Otis is stand-

ing, what is the wavelength of the sound?_____

4. The frequency of sound that you hear is the speed of the sound
divided by the wavelength. What frequency did Otis hear?

_____

5. What is the wavelength of the sound on the side of the dump

truck where Elinor is standing,? _____

6. What frequency did Elinor hear?

_____

7. Complete the chart below.

Listener	Sound wavelength	Sound frequency
Dan		
Otis		
Elinor		

8. Now use the information that you have just gathered and your
understanding of the Doppler effect to explain why Otis heard
the sound differently than Dan.

_____

_____

_____

CHAPTER
21 **VOCABULARY REVIEW WORKSHEET**

Sound Puzzle

After you finish reading Chapter 21, give this puzzle a try!

Fill in each blank with the correct term. Then use the vocabulary words to find the words in the puzzle on the next page.

1. The apparent change in the pitch of a car's horn as it moves past you is a result of the

   _____ effect.

2. When any kind of wave bounces off a barrier, the bouncing back of the wave is called

   _____ . A bounced sound wave is called an

   _____ . This kind of sound wave is the basis for

   _____ , a method whales and bats use to find food.

3. The bending of waves around barriers or through openings is

   called _____ .

4. Each instrument has a unique _____ that is the result of several pitches blending together through interference.

5. The _____ of the note depends on whether it is played softly or loudly, and the

   _____ is how low or high the note sounds.

6. Due to _____ , the vibration of a tuning fork can cause a guitar string to vibrate when the fork is held near the string.

7. The hammer, anvil, and stirrup bones are in the

   _____ ear. The

   _____ ear changes vibrations into

   electrical signals. The _____ ear acts as a funnel for sound waves.

8. Constructive or destructive _____ occurs when sound waves overlap and combine.

9. The _____ is a unit used to express how loud or soft a sound is.

10. A _____ is an undesirable, nonmusical sound that includes a random mix of pitches.

11. An extremely fast airplane can cause an explosive sound

called a _____ boom.

12. _____ sounds have a frequency lower

than 20 Hz, while _____ sounds have a
frequency higher than 20,000 Hz.

13. In a _____ wave, some portions of the
wave are at rest while other portions have a large amplitude.

Search the puzzle below to find each of the words you wrote in the blanks above, and
circle these words in the puzzle. Words may appear horizontally, vertically, or diagonally.

F	B	O	Z	U	M	H	I	Z	I	I	Z	E	D
I	Q	U	A	L	I	T	Y	M	N	R	R	C	I
W	G	T	D	T	O	T	W	F	T	M	E	H	F
V	B	E	W	R	K	U	R	L	E	V	L	O	F
R	U	R	X	A	E	A	D	Z	R	S	P	L	R
X	E	S	T	S	S	H	Y	N	F	U	P	O	A
E	L	N	Z	O	K	C	C	E	E	N	O	C	C
F	D	O	N	N	O	I	S	E	R	S	D	A	T
J	E	I	H	I	O	K	C	Z	E	K	S	T	I
C	C	V	N	C	P	K	Y	H	N	X	Y	I	O
M	I	N	R	R	E	F	L	E	C	T	I	O	N
C	B	N	E	M	I	D	D	L	E	T	Y	N	I
R	E	S	O	N	A	N	C	E	Q	U	I	A	O
P	L	O	E	S	T	A	N	D	I	N	G	P	G

Name _____ Date _____ Class _____

Light Interactions

Complete this worksheet after you finish reading Chapter 22, Section 3.

Light waves can interact with objects or with other light waves in a variety of ways. Complete the table by writing a description or explanation and an example of each kind of light interaction. The first example is provided.

Interaction	Description or explanation	Example
Reflection		A green sweater looks green because green light is reflected off it.
Absorption		
Scattering		
Refraction		
Diffraction		
Interference		

CHAPTER

22 REINFORCEMENT WORKSHEET

Fiona, Private Eye

Complete this worksheet after you finish reading Chapter 22, Section 3.

Fiona wants to be a detective. In order to pass the entrance exam to Private Eye University, she is practicing her spy skills on her friends Jorge, Charles, and Tamika. Reflection is one of the hardest sections on the exam. Use what you have discussed in class to help Fiona learn about the law of reflection.

Figure 1

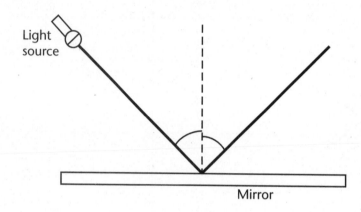

1. Figure 1 in Fiona's notes shows a beam of light hitting and reflecting off a mirror. Label the *normal, incident beam, reflected beam, angle of incidence,* and *angle of reflection* on the diagram.

Fiona knows from the law of reflection that the angle of incidence always equals the angle of reflection. She uses this law to plan a system of mirrors that will allow her to spy on her friends. With her special arrangement of mirrors, Fiona can watch her friends walk by as she hides behind a brick wall.

2. Figure 2 shows the arrangement of mirrors. Using the law of reflection, draw the path of light as it would reflect off each of the mirrors. The normals have been drawn on the reflecting surfaces for you. (Hint: Not all of the mirrors will be used.)

Figure 2

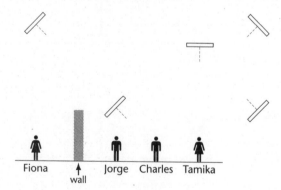

3. Which of her friends is Fiona able to see with her mirrors in their current arrangement?

_____

Name _____ Date _____ Class _____

Puzzle of Light

After you finish reading Chapter 22, give this puzzle a try!

Fill in the blanks below. Then put the letters in the matching numbered squares on the next page to reveal a quote by Albert Einstein.

1. the bending of waves as they pass into a different medium

___ ___ ___ ___ ___ ___ ___ ___ ___
8   12   38

2. energy emitted in the form of EM waves

___ ___ ___ ___ ___ ___ ___ ___
37   7   20

3. the release of energy by particles of matter that have absorbed extra energy

___ ___ ___ ___ ___ ___ ___ ___ ___ ___ ___
32   11   39

4. the material that gives paint its color by absorbing some colors of light and reflecting others

___ ___ ___ ___ ___ ___
6   22

5. occurs when waves overlap and combine

___ ___ ___ ___ ___ ___ ___ ___ ___ ___ ___ ___
34   16

6. the entire range of EM waves, such as light, radio waves, microwaves, and X rays

___ ___ ___ ___ ___ ___ ___ ___ ___ ___ ___ ___
35   17   1

___ ___ ___ ___ ___
31   9

7. the bending of waves around a barrier or through an opening

___ ___ ___ ___ ___ ___ ___ ___ ___ ___ ___
15   26

8. the passing of light through matter

___ ___ ___ ___ ___ ___ ___ ___ ___ ___ ___ ___
13   5   27

9. materials that transmit light easily, without scattering

___ ___ ___ ___ ___ ___ ___ ___ ___
19 28   33

10. waves that are used in radar

___ ___ ___ ___ ___ ___ ___
18   10

11. can be created by combining red, green, and blue light

___ ___ ___ ___ ___ ___ ___
2   23   14

Puzzle of Light, continued

12. the transfer of energy from light waves to particles of matter

— — — — — — — — —
                   4   36

13. when a wave bounces off an object

— — — — — — — — — —
   3   24

14. materials that do not transmit any light

— — — — — — —
21   29

15. materials that transmit and scatter light

— — — — — — — — — —
          25   30

What Albert Einstein said:

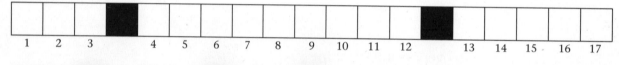

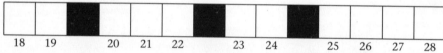

Mirror, Mirror

Complete this worksheet after reading Chapter 23, Section 2.

You will need a straightedge for this activity. Each of the following four illustrations features an object, an image, and a mirror. The optical axis and the focal point are also shown where appropriate.

1. Identify the mirror as plane, convex, or concave. (Circle your answer.)

2. Identify the image as a real or virtual image. (Circle your answer.)

3. For concave and convex mirrors, if the rays are not drawn, draw them into the ray diagram.

plane or convex or concave

real image or virtual image

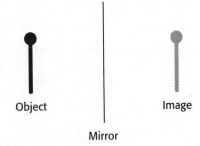

plane or convex or concave

real image or virtual image

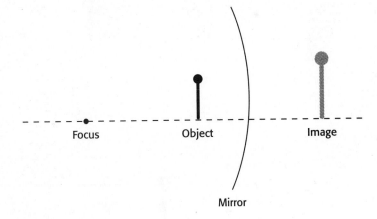

plane or convex or concave

real image or virtual image

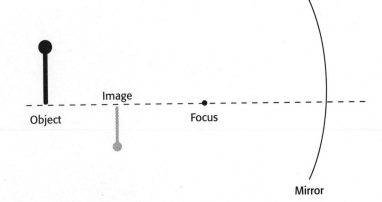

Mirror, Mirror, continued

plane or convex or concave

real image or virtual image

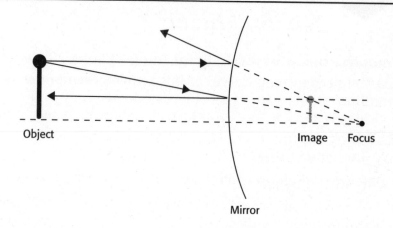

Each illustration below features an object, an image, and a lens. The optical axis and the focal point are also shown.

1. Identify the lens as convex or concave. (Circle your answer.)

2. Identify the image as a real or virtual image. (Circle your answer.)

convex or concave

real image or virtual image

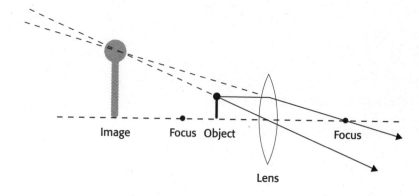

convex or concave

real image or virtual image

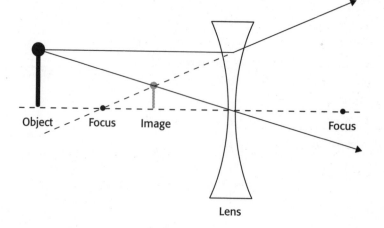

CHAPTER
23 **VOCABULARY REVIEW WORKSHEET**

An Enlightening Puzzle

After finishing Chapter 23, give this puzzle a try!
Use the clues given below to complete the crossword puzzle on the
next page.

ACROSS

2. the opening that lets light into the eye

4. a piece of film on which an interference pattern produces a 3-D image

7. Visible light sources are _____ objects.

8. _____ light is produced when electrons combine with gaseous metal atoms.

11. the back surface of the eye

12. _____ light is light produced by hot objects.

15. The _____ length is the distance between a mirror and its focal point.

17. A(n) _____ is a curved, transparent object that forms an image by refracting light.

18. _____ mirrors produce virtual, upright images that are smaller than the original object.

19. _____ light is produced when certain gases absorb and then release energy.

20. An image formed by a mirror with a flat surface is called a(n) _____ image.

21. A(n) _____ produces intense light of a single color.

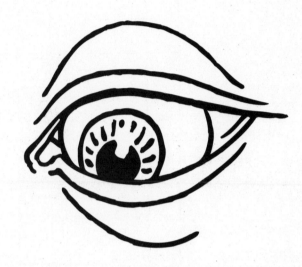

DOWN

1. _____ light is visible light emitted by a phosphor particle when it absorbs energy.

2. _____ mirrors have a flat surface.

3. A visible object that is not a light source is being _____.

5. the opening that lets light into a camera

6. In _____ light, all of the light waves vibrate in the same plane.

9. A straight line drawn outward from the center of a lens or mirror is the _____ axis.

10. Unlike 20 across, light passes through _____ images.

13. _____ lenses are used to correct nearsightedness.

14. the transparent membrane that protects the eye

16. controls the size of the pupil

An Enlightening Puzzle, continued

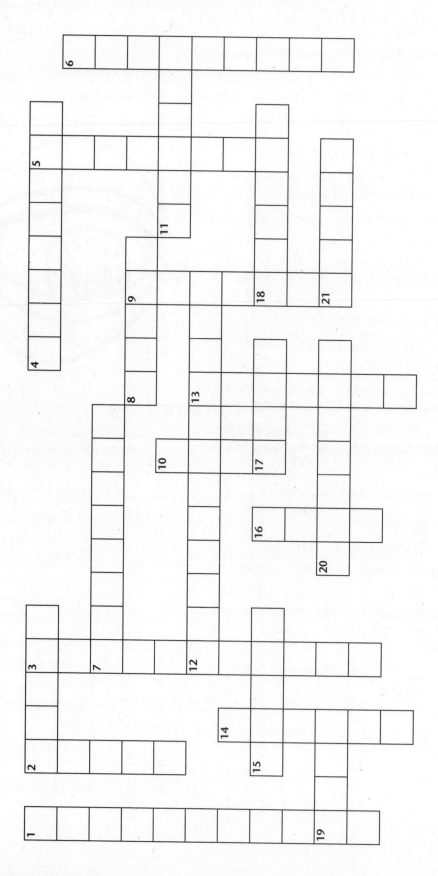

Answer Key

Reinforcement & Vocabulary Review Worksheets

▪ CONTENTS ▪

Name _____ Date _____ Class _____

The Plane Truth

Complete this worksheet after you finish reading Chapter 1, Section 2.
You plan to enter a paper airplane contest sponsored by *Talkin' Physical Science* magazine. The person whose airplane flies the farthest wins a lifetime subscription to the magazine! The week before the contest, you watch an airplane landing at a nearby airport. You notice that the wings of the airplane have flaps, as shown in the illustration at right. The paper airplanes you've been testing do not have wing flaps.

What question would you ask yourself based on these observations? Write your question in the space below for "State the problem." Then tell how you could use the other steps in the scientific method to investigate the problem.

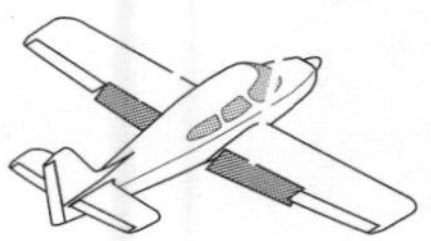

Flaps

1. State the problem.

Accept all reasonable answers. Sample answer: Will a paper airplane with wing flaps fly farther than one without wing flaps?

2. Form a hypothesis.

Accept all reasonable answers. Sample answer: A paper airplane with wing flaps will fly farther than one without wing flaps.

3. Test the hypothesis.

Accept all reasonable answers. Sample answer: I would make two airplanes, identical except one has wing flaps, and the other doesn't. I would then launch both from the same spot several times and measure the length of each flight.

4. Analyze the results.

Accept all reasonable answers. Sample answer: I would find the average distance for flights of airplanes with and without wing flaps.

5. Draw conclusions.

Accept all reasonable answers. Sample answer: If the plane with wing flaps had a longer average flight, I would assume that paper airplanes with wing flaps fly farther; if not, I would assume paper airplanes without flaps fly farther.

CHAPTER 2 REINFORCEMENT WORKSHEET

A Matter of Density

Complete this worksheet after you finish reading Chapter 2, Section 2.

Imagine that you work at a chemical plant. This morning, four different liquid chemicals accidentally spilled into the same tank. Luckily, none of the liquids reacted with each other! Also, you know the liquids do not dissolve in one another, so they must have settled in the tank in four separate layers. The sides of the tank are made of steel, so you can only see the surface of what's inside. But you need to remove the red chemical to use in a reaction later this afternoon. How will you find and remove the red chemical? By finding the chemicals' different densities, of course!

The following liquids were spilled into the tank:

- a green liquid that has a volume of 48 L and a mass of 36 kg
- a blue liquid that has a volume of 144 L and a mass of 129.6 kg
- a red liquid that has a volume of 96 L and a mass of 115.2 kg
- a black liquid that has a volume of 120 L and a mass of 96 kg

1. Calculate the density of each liquid.

   Green liquid: _____ 0.75 kg/L

   Blue liquid: _____ 0.9 kg/L

   Red liquid: _____ 1.2 kg/L

   Black liquid: _____ 0.8 kg/L

2. Determine the order in which the liquids have settled in the tank.

   First (bottom): _____ red

   Second: _____ blue

   Third: _____ black

   Fourth (top): _____ green

3. Use colored pencils to sketch the liquid layers in the container in the diagram on the next page.

4. What kind of property did you use to distinguish between these four chemicals?

   a. a chemical property
   b. a physical property
   c. a liquid property
   d. None of the above

CHAPTER 1 VOCABULARY REVIEW WORKSHEET

The Wide World of Physical Science

After finishing Chapter 1, give this puzzle a try!

ACROSS

1. the ratio of an object's mass to its volume
2. the amount of space something occupies
3. any use of the senses to gather information
4. the application of knowledge, tools, and materials to accomplish tasks
6. measure of the amount of matter in an object
10. Scientists use the _____ System of Units so they can share and compare results.
13. measure of how much surface an object has
15. measure of how hot or cold something is
16. The study of matter and energy is called _____ science.

DOWN

1. A quantity formed from the combination of other measurements is a _____ quantity.
5. a possible explanation or answer to a question
6. A representation of a salt crystal made out of table-tennis balls is a _____ of the crystal.
7. Scientists use the _____ method to solve problems and answer questions.
8. an experimental boat that imitates the way a penguin swims
9. in science, a summary of many experimental results and observations
11. a scientific explanation for a range of hypotheses and observations supported by testing
12. pieces of information acquired through experimentation
14. the basic SI unit of length

Crossword answers:

```
        ¹D E N S I T Y
        E
²V O L U M E
        R
³O B S E R V A T I O N
        ⁴T E C H N O L O G Y
                  ⁵H
⁸I N T E R N A T I O N A L   ¹²D
  C             W           ¹²A R E A
  E           ¹T E M P E R A T U R E
  N                 ¹⁴M
  T               S I
  I             ¹⁵P H Y S I C A L
  F                 ¹⁶
  I
  C
```

Name _____ Date _____ Class _____

CHAPTER 2 **VOCABULARY REVIEW WORKSHEET**

Search for Matter

Complete the puzzle after you finish reading Chapter 2.
Fill in each blank with the correct word. Then find the words in the puzzle. Words in the puzzle can be spelled forward or backward and can be vertical, horizontal, or diagonal.

1. The tendency of an object to resist any change in motion is called ___inertia___ .

2. When water is in a container, the surface of the water is curved. This curve is called the ___meniscus___ .

3. The amount of space occupied by an object is its ___volume___ .

4. Iron ___pyrite___ is also known as fool's gold.

5. The ___mass___ of an object is the amount of matter in the object. The SI unit for expressing this quantity is the ___kilogram___ .

6. The force that causes an object to feel a "pull" toward Earth is called ___gravity___ . The measure of this force is the object's ___weight___ . The SI unit for expressing this force is the ___newton___ .

7. ___Matter___ is anything that has volume and mass.

8. ___Density___ is mass divided by unit volume.

9. A ___chemical___ change occurs when one or more substances are changed into entirely new substances with different properties.

10. Examples of ___physical___ properties are color and odor.

11. A ___characteristic___ property is always the same, whether the sample observed is large or small.

Name _____ Date _____ Class _____

A Matter of Density, continued

5. Now that you know where the red chemical is inside the tank, how can you remove it?

___Accept all reasonable answers. Sample answer: I could open the spigot at___

___the bottom of the tank and let the red liquid out.___

Name _____ Date _____ Class _____

3 REINFORCEMENT WORKSHEET

Make a State-ment

Complete this worksheet after you finish reading Chapter 3, Section 2.
Each figure below shows a container that is meant to hold one state of matter. Identify the state of matter, and write the state on the line below the corresponding figure. Then write each of the descriptions listed below in the correct boxes. Some descriptions may go in more than one box.

Particles are close together.

Particles are held tightly in place by other particles.

Particles break away completely from one another.

changes volume to fill its container

changes shape when placed in a different container

can be used in hydraulic systems

obeys Boyle's law

amount of empty space can change

has definite shape

particles vibrate in place

does not change in volume

has surface tension

State of matter	Description
 Liquid	has surface tension can be used in hydraulic systems changes shape when placed in a different container does not change in volume Particles are close together.
 Gas	Particles break away completely from one another. changes shape when placed in a different container changes volume to fill its container obeys Boyle's law amount of empty space can change
 Solid	Particles are close together. Particles vibrate in place. Particles are held tightly in place by other particles. does not change in volume has definite shape

---

Name _____ Date _____ Class _____

Search for Matter, continued

W	P	F	X	D	E	N	S	I	T	Y	E	P	C
R	E	V	Q	C	J	N	D	Q	W	M	I	I	J
B	P	I	N	E	W	T	O	N	U	A	T	G	K
A	E	F	G	E	X	J	O	L	N	S	I	K	I
G	X	C	J	H	P	O	D	I	I	K	L	L	L
R	Y	M	H	R	T	V	V	R	C	N	Q	P	O
A	S	A	K	E	T	S	E	M	A	E	X	H	G
V	T	S	L	D	M	T	N	F	M	R	U	Y	R
I	W	S	N	N	C	I	M	V	X	T	Z	S	A
T	Y	U	K	A	C	G	C	A	X	I	N	I	M
Y	O	D	R	J	I	N	T	A	T	A	Q	C	M
P	T	A	P	Y	R	I	T	E	L	T	R	A	W
C	H	Z	M	M	P	V	Q	P	B	Z	E	L	B
C	T	Z	C	M	E	N	I	S	C	U	S	R	P

Name _____ Date _____ Class _____

3 VOCABULARY REVIEW WORKSHEET

Know Your States

After you finish Chapter 3, give this puzzle a try!
Use the clues below to complete the crossword puzzle.

ACROSS

3. to change state from a gas to a liquid
6. change of state from a solid to a gas
7. Particles have an orderly arrangement in this type of solid.
10. physical form in which a substance can exist
11. how your body is cooled when you perspire
14. changes shape but doesn't change volume
15. He said that as the volume of a gas increases, its pressure decreases.
16. how molten metal changes into a solid
18. does not change shape when placed in a different container

DOWN

1. measure of the average speed of the particles of a substance
2. to change state from a solid to a liquid
4. Because of surface tension liquids form _____ spherical _____.
5. has no definite shape or volume; conducts electric current
8. Particles are arranged in no particular order in this type of solid.
9. A change of state where energy is given off is called a(n) _____ change.
12. If a substance pours very slowly, it has a high _____.
13. A change of state reaction that energy is endothermic.
15. how hot water changes to steam
17. changes shape and volume to fit container

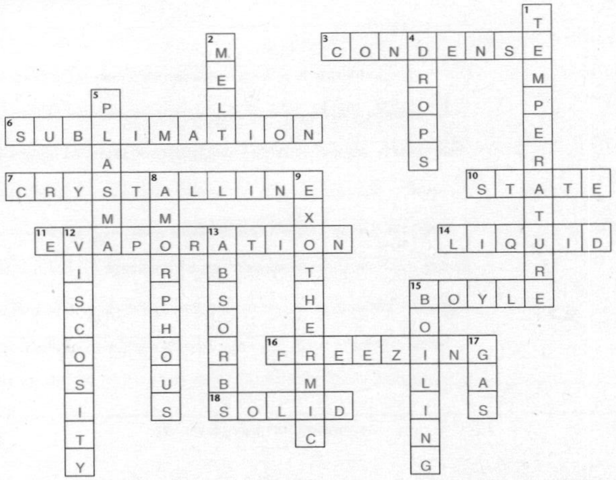

[Crossword puzzle with answers:
3 ACROSS: CONDENSE
2 DOWN: MELTING
5 DOWN: SUBLIMATION
6 ACROSS: SUBLIMATION
7 CRYSTALLINE
8 DOWN: AMORPHOUS
12 DOWN: EVAPORATION
EVAPORATION
SOLID
1 TEMPERATURE
4 PROPERTIES
9 EXOTHERMIC
10 STATE
13 ABSORB
14 LIQUID
15 BOYLE
16 FREEZING
17 GAS
18 SOLID
VISCOSITY]

Name _____ Date _____ Class _____

4 REINFORCEMENT WORKSHEET

It's All Mixed Up

Complete this worksheet after you finish reading Chapter 4, Section 3.
Label each figure below with the type of substance it BEST models:
colloid, compound, element, solution, or suspension.

1. 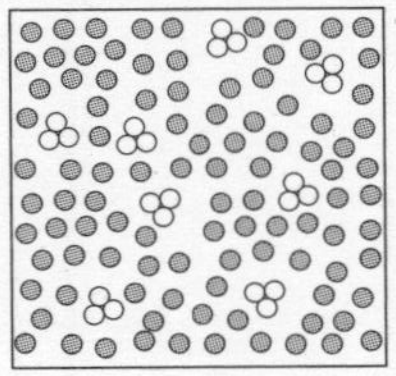 _____ colloid

2. 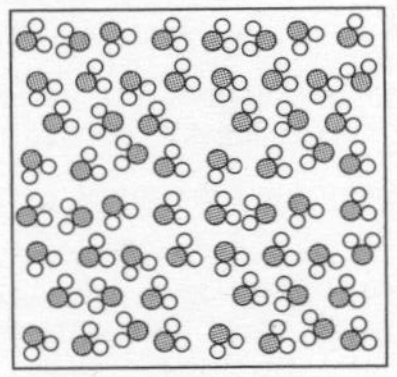 _____ compound

3. 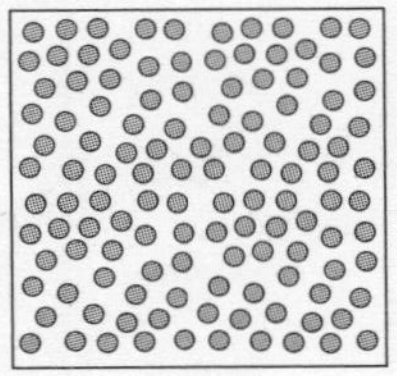 _____ element

4. 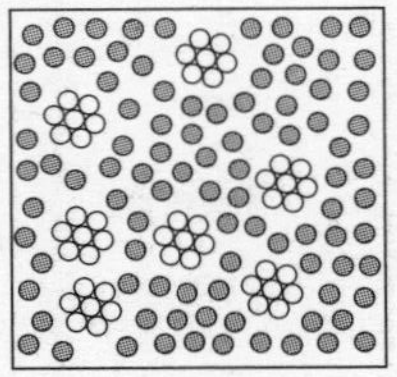 _____ suspension

5. 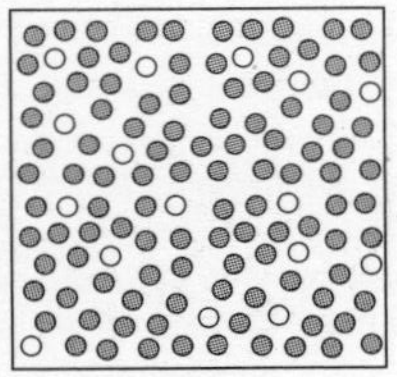 _____ solution

An ELEMENTary Word Puzzle

Give this puzzle a try after you read Chapter 4.

Identify each term described by the clues. Then find and circle each term in the puzzle on the next page. Words may appear forward or backward, horizontally, vertically, or diagonally.

1. solubility — amount of solute needed to make a saturated solution using a given amount of solvent at a certain temperature
2. colloid — mixture in which dispersed particles are too light to settle out
3. solvent — substance in which another is dissolved
4. concentration — can be expressed as grams of solute per milliliter of solvent
5. element — pure substance that cannot be separated into simpler substances by physical or chemical means
6. mixture — two or more substances that are combined physically, not chemically
7. compound — pure substance made up of at least two elements that are chemically combined
8. density — characteristic property measured in grams per cubic centimeter that tells a substance's mass per unit volume
9. metalloid — element that has properties of both metals and nonmetals
10. alloy — solid solution of a metal or a nonmetal dissolved in a metal
11. solute — dissolved substance
12. metal — shiny element; good conductor of thermal energy and electric current
13. suspension — mixture in which particles of one substance are large enough to settle out of another substance
14. solution — brass, salt water, and air, for example
15. nonmetal — element that is a poor conductor of thermal energy and electric current

---

It's All Mixed Up, continued

6. Why did you label the figures on the previous page as you did?

Accept all reasonable answers. Sample answer: In Figure 3, the particles were identical and part of the same substance, so it had to be an element. Figure 2 was a compound because the particles were identical but made of two different substances. The other three figures were mixtures because each contained two different types of particles. Figure 4 had the largest clumps of the solute, so it was a suspension. Figure 1 had the next-largest clumps of the second substance, making it a colloid. Figure 5 had the most homogeneous mix of the two substances, making it a solution.

Professor Jumble's Confusion

In her lab, Professor Jumble has four shelves labeled "Suspensions," "Solutions," "Compounds," and "Colloids," respectively. Last night, the professor set one beaker of clear liquid on each of the four shelves. When the professor walked into her lab this morning, all four beakers were on the same shelf, and she didn't know which was which. She tested each beaker, and the results are below.

Use the test results to help Professor Jumble unjumble the beakers, and write the identity of each liquid in the blanks.

Beaker A: _solution_	Beaker B: _compound_
• Light passes right through. • Particles do not separate in a centrifuge or a filter. • Upon heating, the liquid evaporates, and a crystal powder remains.	• Light passes right through. • Particles do not separate in a centrifuge or a filter. • Upon heating, the liquid evaporates, but no residue remains. • The particles could not be separated by any other physical changes.
Beaker C: _suspension_	Beaker D: _colloid_
• Liquid scatters light. • Liquid centrifuged into two different-colored layers. • Particles were left behind in the filter.	• Liquid scatters light. • Liquid passes through a filter without leaving a residue.

Name _____ Date _____ Class _____

An ELEMENTary Word Puzzle, continued

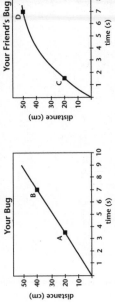

Name _____ Date _____ Class _____

CHAPTER 5

REINFORCEMENT WORKSHEET

Bug Race

Complete this worksheet after you finish reading Chapter 5, Section 1.
You and a friend are having a bug race. You measure the distance your pet bugs travel along a straight race track and record their time as they race. The results are plotted in the graphs below. Take a look at the two graphs. Then answer the questions that follow.

Your Bug

Your Friend's Bug

1. Look at Point A. What distance has your bug traveled so far? _____ 20 cm

2. How long did it take your bug to travel that distance? _____ 3.5 s

3. To determine your bug's average speed while traveling from the starting line to Point A, divide the distance traveled by the time it took to travel that distance:

   average speed = $\dfrac{\text{distance traveled}}{\text{elapsed time}}$ = $\dfrac{20\ cm}{3.5\ s}$ = 5.7 cm/s

4. Now look at Point B. What is the distance from Point A to Point B? _____ 20 cm

5. How long did it take your bug to travel from Point A to Point B? _____ 3.5 s

6. Calculate your bug's average speed from Point A to Point B.
   $\dfrac{20\ cm}{3.5\ s}$ = 5.7 cm/s

7. Compare the graphs of your bug and your friend's bug. Which bug was traveling at a constant speed? Explain.

   My bug was traveling at a constant speed. For my bug, averge speed did not change over time, so

   the graph of distance traveled over time is a straight line.

CHAPTER

5 REINFORCEMENT WORKSHEET

A Weighty Problem

Complete this worksheet after you finish reading Chapter 5, Section 4.

Pictured below are two measurement devices, A and B.

Weight or Mass?
• spring scale
• measure of gravitational force exerted on an object
• constant on Earth
• changes when gravitational force changes
• expressed in newtons
• six times less on the moon than on the Earth

Weight or Mass?
• balance
• amount of matter in an object
• constant on Earth
• never changes
• measured in grams
• remains the same when gravitational force changes

A.

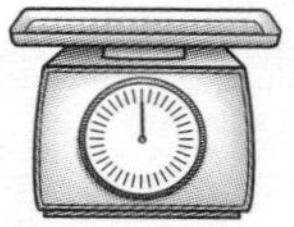

spring scale

B.

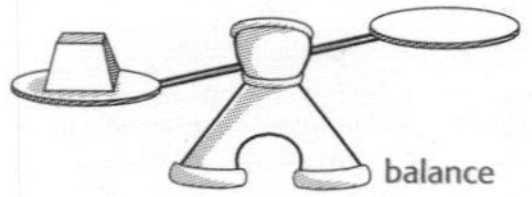

balance

1. Determine whether each device measures *mass* or *weight*, and circle the correct term in each box.

2. The following list contains information that relates to either *mass* or *weight*. Write each of the bulleted items in the correct boxes above. Some information may go in more than one box.

- balance
- spring scale
- measure of gravitational force exerted on an object
- constant on Earth
- measured in grams

- changes when gravitational force changes
- never changes
- expressed in newtons
- remains the same when gravitational force changes
- six times less on the moon than on the Earth

CHAPTER

5 REINFORCEMENT WORKSHEET

Friction Action

Complete this worksheet after you finish reading Chapter 5, Section 3.

Steve challenged his little sister Jenny to a problem: Use all four types of friction to get home from school as quickly and as safely as possible. He reminded her that the four types of friction are sliding, rolling, static, and fluid. Here's what Jenny did:

> Jenny hopped on her bicycle after school. **What a perfect day to be cycling—the sun was shining, there was a slight breeze in the air, and the temperature was a comfortable 27°C.** Jenny got on the bike path and began pedaling as fast as she could. The wheels of the bicycle were turning at a furious pace. **And the faster Jenny pedaled, the stronger the breezy air blew in her face.** All of a sudden, she came across a huge tree branch that had fallen on the path. Jenny slammed on her brakes and stopped just in time to avoid hitting the fallen branch. **That was a close call!** She got off of her bike and tried to push the branch to the side of the path so that others would not get hurt, but it was too heavy to budge. Jenny continued on her journey and got home safely in record time.

Did Jenny meet Steve's challenge? Explain.

Sample answer: Yes; Jenny met Steve's challenge. The friction between the

turning wheels of her bike and the ground was rolling friction. The air blowing

against Jenny's face as she pedaled faster caused fluid friction. The sliding

of the brakes on the wheels of the bicycle was an example of sliding friction.

And the friction that prevented her from moving the heavy branch was static

friction. _____

_____

_____

_____

Name _____ Date _____ Class _____

Falling Fast

Complete this worksheet after you finish reading Chapter 6, Section 1.

A stone rolls off a 150 m cliff. The partially completed table below shows the distance fallen and the velocity of the stone for the first few seconds of its fall.

1. Use the formula below to calculate the velocity of the stone at the end of each second. Remember that acceleration due to gravity is 9.8 m/s/s. Record the answers in the table in the column labeled "Velocity." The first few calculations are done for you.

Notice that the stone's initial velocity is 0 m/s. The velocity at the end of one second is the initial velocity plus the change in velocity due to gravity:

velocity = initial velocity + change in velocity

Since the initial velocity is 0 m/s, we can ignore it.

velocity = change in velocity

$= \Delta v$

= (acceleration due to gravity) × (time)

Time (s)	Velocity (m/s)	Distance fallen during this second (m)
0	0	0
1	$\Delta v = 9.8 \times 1 = 9.8$	4.9
2	$\Delta v = 9.8 \times 2 = 19.6$	4.9 + 9.8 = 14.7
3	29.4	4.9 + 9.8 + 9.8 = 24.5
4	39.2	4.9 + 3(9.8) = 34.3
5	49.0	4.9 + 4(9.8) = 44.1
6	58.8	4.9 + 5(9.8) = 53.9

2. Do you see the pattern in the calculations for the third column? Calculate the distance fallen in each second, and record the two remaining values in the column labeled "Distance fallen during this second" in the table.

Name _____ Date _____ Class _____

Penny's Puns

After you finish Chapter 5, give this puzzle a try!

Oh no! Penny Punster's computer mixed up her physical science dictionary with her dictionary of puns. The computer paired the terms related to forces with her goofy definitions, and it paired her pun-related terms with the real definitions. Help Penny unscramble the mismatched pairs and get her dictionaries back in order. The first one has been done for you!

c **1. farce:** a push or pull

f **2. grubby tea:** force of attraction between objects due to mass

k **3. freak sheen:** force opposing motion between touching surfaces

g **4. fellow's city:** speed in a particular direction

i **5. sty tic:** friction that disappears when an object starts moving

l **6. exhilaration:** rate at which velocity changes

e **7. mow shun:** changing position over time

n **8. spyed:** rate at which an object moves

a **9. bell lanced:** forces producing a net force of zero

h **10. net for us:** result of combined forces on an object

m **11. wade:** measure of the force of gravity on an object

j **12. mace:** amount of matter in an object

q **13. roe link:** friction between wheels and the floor

p **14. Libra can't:** reduces friction

d **15. flu ad:** friction that slows down a swimmer

b **16. now ten:** unit used to express force

o **17. sly ding:** friction that makes brakes work

a. balanced: a ringer on a stick

b. newton: used to be nine

c. force: slapstick

d. fluid: influenza commercial

e. motion: lawn-cutting avoidance

f. gravity: dirty English drink

g. velocity: guy's town

h. net force: mesh that's ours

i. static: pigpen twitch

j. mass: spiked medieval war club

k. friction: weird shininess

l. acceleration: thrill

m. weight: slowly walk into the water

n. speed: played secret agent

o. sliding: sneaky dent

p. lubricant: the sign between Virgo and Scorpio won't work

q. rolling: fish egg connection

CHAPTER 6

VOCABULARY REVIEW WORKSHEET

A Matter of Real Gravity

After you finish Chapter 6, give this puzzle a try!

Use the clues given to fill in the blanks below. Then copy the numbered letters into the corresponding squares on the next page to reveal a quotation attributed to Galileo.

1. When gravity is the only force acting on an object, the object is in
   F R E E   F A L L .
   52   47   29

2. Because of free fall, astronauts appear this way in orbit.
   W E I G H T L E S S
   40   51   2   13   44

3. The velocity at which a falling object travels when the force of air resistance exactly matches the downward force of gravity is called the
   T E R M I N A L   V E L O C I T Y .
   12   46   17   25   8   19   49   30

4. The unbalanced force that causes an object to move in a circular path is called a _____ force.
   C E N T R I P E T A L
   32   22   42   1   39

5. Sir Isaac Newton is famous for his three laws of
   M O T I O N .
   11   54   38   33   26

6. Newton's third law states that objects exert _____ and _____ forces on each other.
   E Q U A L   O P P O S I T E
   34   16   23   18   31

7. The curved path traveled by a thrown baseball is known as
   P R O J E C T I L E   M O T I O N .
   10   45   27   35   15   37

8. The acceleration of a falling object is caused by the force of
   G R A V I T Y .
   21   53   48

9. _____ is the tendency of an object to resist any change in its motion.
   I N E R T I A
   50   24   56   3

10. A moving object's _____ depends on the object's mass and velocity.
    M O M E N T U M
    55   9   43   57

Falling Fast, continued

3. After 2 seconds, the stone will have fallen a total of 19.6 m (distance after first second + distance during second second). How far will the stone have fallen after 5 seconds? (Use the space below for your calculations.)

   4.9 m + 14.7 m + 24.5 m + 34.3 m + 44.1 m = 122.5 m

   After 5 seconds, the stone will have fallen
   __122.5_____ m.

4. Approximately when will the stone hit the ground? Explain your reasoning.

   It will take between 5 and 6 seconds to hit the ground. At the end of

   5 seconds, the stone will have fallen 122.5 m. It takes 6 seconds for the

   stone to fall 176.4 m, but the cliff is only 150 m high. Therefore, the

   stone will hit the ground some time between 5 and 6 seconds after rolling

   off the cliff.

   _____

   _____

5. If a much heavier stone rolled off the same cliff, would it hit the ground more quickly? Explain.

   No; a heavier stone would hit the ground in the same amount of time.

   Objects fall to the ground at the same rate because the acceleration due

   to gravity is the same for all objects.

   _____

Name _____ Date _____ Class _____

CHAPTER 7

REINFORCEMENT WORKSHEET

Building Up Pressure

Complete this worksheet after you finish reading Chapter 7.

1. Below is a diagram of a balloon that has just been released. Identify the areas of high and low pressure, and label them on the diagram.

Low pressure

High pressure

Low pressure

Low pressure

Air outflow

Thrust

2. Why does air rush out of the balloon when you release it?

Sample answer: The air inside the balloon is under a higher pressure than

the air outside of the balloon. Fluids flow from regions of high pressure to

regions of low pressure. The air under high pressure will rush out of the

balloon until the pressure inside the balloon equals the pressure outside

the balloon.

_____

_____

_____

Name _____ Date _____ Class _____

A Matter of Real Gravity, continued

11. The fluid friction that opposes the motion of objects through air is known as

   A I R   R E S I S T A N C E .
   14   5 20 28 41 36   7

I		H	A	V	E		N	E	V	E	R		M	E	T		A
1	2	3	4	5	6	7	8	9	10	11	12	13			14		

M	A	N		S	O		I	G	N	O	R	A	N	T		T	H	A	T
15	16	17	18	19	20	21	22	23	24	25	26	27	28			29	30		

I		C	O	U	L	D		N	O	T		L	E	A	R	N
31	32	33	34	35	36	37	38	39	40	41	42	43

S	O	M	E	T	H	I	N	G		F	R	O	M		H	I	M	.
44	45	46	47	48	49	50	51	52	53	54	55	56	57

CHAPTER 7 ▸ VOCABULARY REVIEW WORKSHEET

Go with the Flow

After completing Chapter 7, give this puzzle a try!
Fill in the blanks in the clues below. Then use the clues to complete the puzzle on the next page.

Clues

1. _____Archimedes_____ discovered that the buoyant force depends on the weight of the displaced fluid.

2. _____Bernoulli_____ described the connection between fluid speed and pressure.

3. A swim _____bladder_____ controls a fish's overall density.

4. _____Buoyant_____ force is the upward force exerted on any object in a fluid.

5. The layer of gases surrounding the Earth is called the atmosphere _____.

6. A _____fluid_____ is something that flows.

7. _____Lift_____ is the upward force due to fluid flow around an airplane wing.

8. The amount of matter in a certain volume divided by the volume is _____density_____.

9. A fluid force that opposes motion is called _____drag_____.

10. One newton per square meter is a _____pascal_____.

11. A _____hydraulic_____ device uses a liquid to transmit pressure from one point to another.

12. An irregular fluid flow is _____turbulence_____.

13. To _____displace_____ is to move into something else's location by pushing it aside.

14. _____Pressure_____ is the amount of force exerted on a given area divided by the area.

15. The forward force from a plane's engine is _____thrust_____.

Building Up Pressure, continued

3. Is the pressure of the stream of air exiting the balloon different from the pressure of the air around the balloon? Explain in terms of Bernoulli's principle.

Yes; Bernoulli's principle says that as the speed of a moving fluid increases, its pressure decreases. The air exiting the balloon is moving faster than the air around the balloon. That means the pressure of the air exiting the bal-

loon is lower than the pressure of the air around the balloon.

_____

_____

4. Add an arrow to the diagram on the previous page to show the direction of the air coming out of the balloon. Add another arrow indicating the direction the balloon is pushed by the exiting air. Label the first arrow "Air outflow," and label the second arrow "Thrust."

5. If you attach some weight to the balloon, it might not be able to fly. Use the terms *weight*, *thrust*, and *lift* to explain.

Sample answer: The added *weight* would mean a greater downward pull

of gravity on the balloon. For the balloon to fly, there must be enough

thrust to create enough *lift* to counter the downward pull of gravity. If the

pull of gravity is greater than the *lift*, the balloon won't fly.

_____

_____

_____

Name _____ Date _____ Class _____

Go with the Flow, continued

How many chapter concepts can you find in the block of letters below? Use the clues on the previous page to help you. Words may appear horizontally, vertically, diagonally, or backward.

T	U	R	B	U	L	E	N	C	E	M	E	Z	C	E	E	K
C	A	S	O	Q	V	H	Y	D	R	A	U	L	I	C	D	I
P	R	E	S	S	U	R	E	G	Y	Q	A	K	J	E	X	Q
O	Z	D	Q	G	R	T	N	A	Y	O	U	S	B	R	Z	N
B	K	D	F	P	D	E	N	S	I	T	Y	S	L	K	I	
T	P	C	H	D	G	C	T	P	X	T	E	E	J	A	Z	J
A	S	J	A	W	B	N	S	G	T	R	D	R	Z	D	F	D
O	T	U	A	J	A	F	G	F	P	E	S	X	M	D	S	N
G	I	M	R	Z	Z	Q	I	M	J	C	X	S	E	U	I	
S	E	V	O	H	T	L	O	I	B	H	T	M	C	R	D	L
Q	P	L	B	S	T	C	H	L	H	B	J	P	G	I	L	
X	Y	R	W	G	P	C	I	O	N	F	T	D	A	J	S	U
U	R	M	N	D	R	H	I	S	F	F	U	A	S	I	P	O	N
C	T	T	I	A	R	E	D	N	J	J	A	C	F	L	N
Q	M	U	V	Q	A	R	J	R	R	W	H	R	A	P	A	R
V	L	L	H	U	Y	R	M	W	E	A	R	R	L	P	C	E
F	Q	J	I	M	F	J	O	U	H	G	F	S	L	E	B

Name _____ Date _____ Class _____

Mechanical Advantage and Efficiency

Complete this worksheet after you have finished reading Chapter 8, Section 3. Carlita, Tom, and Jamal are having a contest to see who can build the best pulley. After they finish constructing the pulleys, they measure the input and output forces as well as the input and output work. Below is a chart with the results. Help the three students calculate the mechanical advantage and the mechanical efficiency of each of the pulleys.

1. What is the output force of Tom's pulley? __60 N__
2. What is the input force of Tom's pulley? __15 N__
3. Divide the output force by the input force. __4__
4. Your answer for item 3 is the mechanical advantage for Tom's pulley. Record this value on the chart below. Calculate the mechanical advantage of the other two pulleys in the same way, and record these values on the chart.

5. What is the output work of Carlita's pulley? __3 N__
6. What is the input work of Carlita's pulley? __4 N__
7. Divide the output work by the input work. __0.75__
8. Multiply your answer for item 7 by 100%. __75%__
9. Your answer for item 8 is the mechanical efficiency for Carlita's pulley. Record this value on the chart. Calculate the mechanical efficiency of the other two pulleys in the same way, and fill in these values in the chart.

	Force (N)		Work (J)		Mechanical advantage	Mechanical efficiency
	Input	Output	Input	Output		
Carlita	4	8	4	3	2	75%
Tom	15	60	12	6	4	50%
Jamal	25	100	10	9	4	90%

10. Based on your calculations, whose pulley won the contest? Explain your reasoning.
Jamal's pulley is the best because his has the highest values for both mechanical advantage and mechanical efficiency. This means that he will get more output work for the effort he puts in and that his pulley has relatively little friction.

CHAPTER 8 VOCABULARY REVIEW WORKSHEET

Searching for Work

Now that you have read Chapter 8, give this word search a try!
After filling in the blanks, find the words in the puzzle on the next page.

1. The unit used to express work is the __joule__.
2. A __screw__ is an inclined plane that is wrapped in a spiral.
3. __Power__ is the rate at which work is done.
4. __Work__ occurs when a force causes an object to move in the direction of the force.
5. The work you do on a machine is called the work __input__.
6. An __inclined plane__ is a simple machine that is a straight, slanted surface.
7. The mechanical __advantage__ of a machine compares the input force with the output force.
8. All machines are constructed from six __simple__ machines.
9. When two kinds of pulleys are used together, the system is called a __block and tackle__.
10. A __lever__ is a simple machine consisting of a bar that pivots at a fixed point.
11. A __machine__ is a device that helps make work easier by changing the size or direction of force.
12. A __wedge__ is a double inclined plane that moves.
13. Machines that are made up of two or more simple machines are called __compound__ machines.
14. A __wheel and axle__ is a simple machine consisting of two circular objects of different sizes.
15. A __pulley__ consists of a grooved wheel that holds a rope or a cable.
16. The work done by a machine is called the work __output__.
17. The fixed point at which a lever pivots is called a __fulcrum__.
18. Two kinds of pulleys are __fixed__ pulleys and __movable__ pulleys.
19. The unit used to express power is the __watt__.
20. Mechanical __efficiency__ is a comparison of a machine's work output with the work input.

CHAPTER 8 REINFORCEMENT WORKSHEET

Finding Machines in Everyday Life

Complete this worksheet after you have finished reading Chapter 8, Section 3.
In Chapter 8 you learned about work and how machines can help make all kinds of work easier. You saw examples of simple machines and compound machines. In the drawing below, find as many machines as you can, and classify them as simple or compound. For each simple machine, write what type of simple machine it is.

Simple Machines	Compound Machines
door knob, wheel and axle	can opener
window blind cord, pulley	scissors
knife, wedge	stand mixer
faucet, screwdriver, wheel and axle	coffee maker
bottle opener, lever	toaster
jar lid, screw	refrigerator
screw, screw	dishwasher
ramp, inclined plane	stove

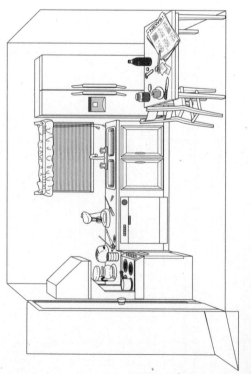

Name _____ Date _____ Class _____

Searching for Work, continued

In the puzzle below, find the words from the blanks on the previous page. Words may appear horizontally, vertically, or diagonally.

F	B	P	B	W	A	T	T	N	C	S	K	R	E	E
F	U	L	Y	Q	O	U	C	M	I	E	L	N	R
E	P	L	O	L	U	E	P	C	W	V	P	A	R	W
F	C	S	C	C	L	F	H	D	E	M	L	E	E	W
F	O	A	F	R	K	E	B	L	I	P	F	M	E	E
I	M	X	I	J	U	A	Y	S	D	H	K	W	H	D
C	P	F	X	F	M	N	E	J	O	U	L	E	G
I	O	D	E	X	T	A	N	D	O	P	J	H	Q	E
E	U	W	D	W	S	I	E	M	T	Z	O	H	C	D
N	N	V	E	T	L	N	D	U	O	A	L	W	C	U
C	D	R	U	C	I	J	S	P	U	V	C	T	E	F
Y	C	P	N	H	O	U	T	P	U	T	A	K	D	R
S	N	I	C	W	O	R	K	X	Q	K	D	B	L	U
I	Z	A	V	A	D	V	A	N	T	A	G	E	L	E
D	M	W	H	E	E	L	A	N	D	A	X	L	E

Name _____ Date _____ Class _____

See What I Saw

Complete this worksheet after you finish reading Chapter 9, Section 2.

In each of the following diagrams, a boy and a girl of equal mass sit on opposite sides of a seesaw. The arrows indicate direction of movement. Take a few moments to look over the figures, and then circle the statement that correctly describes the transfer of energy for each figure.

1.

a. The girl's potential energy increases as the boy's kinetic energy increases.

b. The boy's potential energy and the girl's potential energy decrease.

c. The girl's kinetic energy increases as the boy's potential energy increases.

d. The kinetic and potential energies of the boy and the girl are equal.

2.

a. The girl's potential energy increases as the boy's kinetic energy increases.

b. The boy's potential energy and the girl's potential energy decrease.

c. The girl's kinetic energy increases as the boy's potential energy increases.

d. The kinetic and potential energies of the boy and the girl are equal.

3.

a. The girl's potential energy increases as the boy's kinetic energy increases.

b. The boy's potential energy and the girl's potential energy decrease.

c. The girl's kinetic energy increases as the boy's potential energy increases.

d. The kinetic and potential energies of the boy and the girl are equal.

4. Remember that mechanical energy is the sum of kinetic and potential energy. What happens to the amount of mechanical energy in the boy in Figure 3 as his potential and kinetic energies change?

The mechanical energy of the boy stays the same.

CHAPTER 9 **REINFORCEMENT WORKSHEET**

Energetic Cooking

Complete this worksheet after you finish reading Chapter 9, Section 2.

Jerry is busy preparing for breakfast. Little does he know that energy conversions are taking place every step of the way! Identify the energy conversion that takes place after each of Jerry's actions, and describe the energy conversion in the space provided.

1. Jerry dusted off his solar-powered juice maker and placed it in direct sunlight so he could make freshly squeezed orange juice to go with his breakfast.

Light energy is converted to electrical energy in the solar panel, and electri-

cal energy is converted to mechanical energy in the juicer.

2. Jerry plugged in the electric frying pan, turned it on "high," and waited a few minutes while the pan heated.

Electrical energy from the outlet is converted into thermal energy in the

frying pan.

3. When the indicator light turned on, Jerry was ready to cook.

Electrical energy from the outlet is converted into light energy.

4. He mixed up his secret recipe, poured it into the pan, and listened as the mixture sizzled.

Thermal energy from the frying pan is converted into sound.

5. As the mixture heated, it thickened and started to change color.

Thermal energy in the frying pan is converted into chemical energy.

6. When the mixture seemed cooked, Jerry placed it on his plate and turned off the frying pan. Next he added cold water to the frying pan, which made a giant "whooshing" noise.

Thermal energy in the frying pan is converted into sound energy.

BONUS QUESTION: What energy conversion takes place in Jerry's body after he eats the breakfast he has prepared?

Chemical energy is converted into thermal energy and kinetic energy.

CHAPTER 9 **VOCABULARY REVIEW WORKSHEET**

Exercising Your Potential

Complete the following puzzle after you finish reading Chapter 9. Use each of the following clues to find the correct energy-related word, and write the word in the spaces provided. Then on the next page, put the numbered letters into the matching numbered squares to reveal a quotation by Nancy Newhall.

1. a force that opposes motion between surfaces that are touching

F R I C T I O N
35   9

2. energy resources that formed from the buried remains of plants and animals that lived millions of years ago

F O S S I L   F U E L S
14   38

3. the energy of motion

K I N E T I C
3   20

4. the process that captures the sun's energy for food making in plants

P H O T O S Y N T H E S I S
11   21 33   10

5. energy resources that cannot be replaced after they are used

N O N R E N E W A B L E
19   8

6. units used to express energy

J O U L E S
30   40

7. a well-defined group of objects that transfer energy between one another

C L O S E D   S Y S T E M
1   32   17

8. the sum of kinetic and potential energies

M E C H A N I C A L   E N E R G Y
28   15   18

9. potential energy dependent upon an object's weight and distance from the Earth's surface

G R A V I T A T I O N A L
28   37

10. the ability to do work

E N E R G Y
34   39

11. resources that can be used and replaced in nature over a relatively short period of time

R E N E W A B L E
6

Name _____ Date _____ Class _____

CHAPTER 10 REINFORCEMENT WORKSHEET

Feel the Heat

Complete this worksheet after you have finished reading Chapter 10, Section 2. Beneath the description, write the method of heating that is taking place. (conduction, convection, or radiation)

1. One heater located in the deep end warms Carlos's entire swimming pool.

convection

2. The sunlight shines directly on Janet's desk but not on Carlos's desk. Both Janet and Carlos are near the window, yet Janet feels much warmer than Carlos.

radiation

3. Carlos places a spoon in a steaming hot bowl of soup. Minutes later, the hot handle burns his fingers.

conduction

OUCH!

Name _____ Date _____ Class _____

Exercising Your Potential, continued

12. the energy of shape or position
P O T E N T I A L
 ‾2‾   ‾13‾

13. a change of one form of energy into another
C O N V E R S I O N
‾23‾ ‾4‾   ‾27‾

14. produced when two or more nuclei join together or when the nucleus of one atom splits apart
N U C L E A R   E N E R G Y
‾16‾ ‾24‾   ‾12‾

15. a natural resource that can be converted by humans into other forms of energy in order to do useful work
E N E R G Y   R E S O U R C E
  ‾25‾   ‾36‾ ‾31‾

16. a comparison of the amount of energy before a conversion with the amount of useful energy after a conversion
E N E R G Y
 ‾22‾
E F F I C I E N C Y
‾29‾ ‾26‾

Nancy Newhall's Quotation:

C	O	N	S	E	R	V	A	T	I	O	N	■	I	S
1	2	3	4	5	6	7	8	9	10	11	12	13	14	

H	U	M	A	N	I	T	Y	■	C	A	R	I	N	G
15	16	17	18	19	20	21	22	23	24	25	26	27	28	

F	O	R	■	T	H	E	■	F	U	T	U	R	E	■ .
29	30	31	32	33	34	35	36	37	38	39	40			

Riddle Me This, continued

1. C O N D U C T I O N
2. C H A N G E   O F   S T A T E
3. S P E C I F I C   H E A T   C A P A C I T Y
4. G R E E N H O U S E   E F F E C T
5. C O N V E C T I O N
6. T H E R M A L   E N E R G Y
7. H E A T
8. T H E R M A L   P O L L U T I O N
9. C O N D U C T O R
10. H E A T   E N G I N E
11. T H E R M A L   E X P A N S I O N
12. R A D I A T I O N
13. T E M P E R A T U R E
14. I N S U L A T O R
15. A B S O L U T E   Z E R O
16. S T A T E S   O F   M A T T E R

Feel the Heat, continued

4. Carlos licks a juice pop that he has just removed from the freezer. The tip of his tongue freezes and sticks to the icy-cold treat.

_____conduction_____

5. When Janet sits near the campfire, her face feels hot even though her back feels cold.

_____radiation_____

6. When Janet wins first place in the science-fair competition, Carlos shakes her hand. Her hand feels cold to him.

_____conduction_____

7. Bubbles of liquid in Carlos's lava lamp are heated at the lamp's base. The bubbles then rise to the top. They fall after being cooled.

_____convection_____

Name _____ Date _____ Class _____

REINFORCEMENT WORKSHEET

Atomic Timeline

Complete this worksheet after you have finished reading Chapter 11, Section 1.
The table below contains a number of statements connected to major discoveries in the development of atomic theory.

1. In each box, write the name of the scientist(s) associated with the statement. Choose from among the following scientists:

- Democritus 440 B.C.
- Thomson 1897
- Bohr 1913
- Rutherford 1911
- Dalton 1803
- Schrödinger and Heisenberg twentieth century

2. On a separate sheet of paper, construct a timeline, and label the following: 440 B.C., 1803, 1897, 1911, 1913, and the twentieth century. Cut out the boxes below along the dotted lines, and glue each box of information at the correct point along your timeline.

There are small, negatively charged particles inside an atom. 1897 (Thomson)	Electron paths cannot be predicted. twentieth century (Schrödinger and Heisenberg)
There is a small, dense, positively charged nucleus. 1911 (Rutherford)	Electrons travel in definite paths. 1913 (Bohr)
Most of an atom's mass is in the nucleus. 1911 (Rutherford)	Electrons move in empty space in the atom. 1911 (Rutherford)
Electrons jump between levels from path to path. 1913 (Bohr)	His theory of atomic structure led to the "plum-pudding" model. 1897 (Thomson)
He conducted the cathode-ray tube experiment. 1897 (Thomson)	Electrons are found in electron clouds, not paths. twentieth century (Schrödinger and Heisenberg)
Atoms of different elements are different. 1803 (Dalton)	Atoms of the same element are exactly alike. 1803 (Dalton)
Atoms contain mostly empty space. 1911 (Rutherford)	Atoms constantly move. 440 B.C. (Democritus)
Atoms are small, hard particles. 440 B.C. (Democritus)	All substances are made of atoms. 1803 (Dalton)
He conducted experiments in combining elements. 1803 (Dalton)	He conducted the gold foil experiment. 1911 (Rutherford)
Atoms are "uncuttable." 440 B.C. (Democritus)	Elements combine in specific proportions. 1803 (Dalton)

Name _____ Date _____ Class _____

VOCABULARY REVIEW WORKSHEET

Atomic Anagrams

Try this anagram after you have finished Chapter 11. Use the definitions below to unscramble the vocabulary words.

1. weighted average of the masses of all naturally occurring isotopes of the same element   MICTOA SAMS   **atomic mass**

2. the building blocks of matter   MOATS   **atoms**

3. unifying scientific explanation supported by testing   RYTHOE   **theory**

4. positively charged particle in the atom   TORPNO   **proton**

5. made up of protons and neutrons   UCSELUN   **nucleus**

6. particle in the atom that has no charge   TRONUNE   **neutron**

7. atoms with the same number of protons but different numbers of neutrons   SOOTPIES   **isotopes**

8. negatively charged particle in the atom   CLEENROT   **electron**

9. number of protons in a nucleus   MICOTA BRUMEN   **atomic number**

10. representation of an object or system   OLDEM   **model**

11. regions where electrons are likely to be found   RENECTOL SCUDLO   **electron clouds**

12. SI unit used to express the mass of atomic particles   MUA   **amu**

13. sum of protons and neutrons   SAMS BRUNEM   **mass number**

Name _____ Date _____ Class _____

Placing All Your Elements on the Table, continued

Answer the following questions using the periodic table on the previous page.

14. The alkaline-earth metals react similarly because they all have the same number of electrons in their outer energy level. Which group contains the alkaline-earth metals?

They are in Group 2.

15. How many electrons are in the outer energy level of the atoms of alkaline-earth metals? ____2____

16. Hydrogen is in a different color than the rest of the elements in Group 1. Give an example of how hydrogen's characteristics set it apart from other Group 1 elements.

Sample answer: The alkali metals are solids, while hydrogen is a gas at

room temperature.

17. What is the name for the group of elements that are particularly unreactive?

They are called the noble gases.

18. Except for the metalloids, what do all of the elements on the right side of the zigzag line have in common?
a. They are not very reactive.   c. They are all metals.
b. They are all nonmetals.   d. They are all very reactive.

19. Lanthanide and actinide elements are transition metals.

True or False? (Circle one.)

Imagine you are a scientist who has just discovered a new element. The element has an atomic number of 113, and it has three electrons in the outer energy level of each atom.

20. Where would you place this new element in the periodic table?

I would place it in Group 13.

21. Which element would have properties most similar to the new element?
a. hydrogen   **c.** boron
b. beryllium   d. carbon

22. What name would you suggest for this new element?

Accept all answers.

40   HOLT SCIENCE AND TECHNOLOGY

Name _____ Date _____ Class _____

Placing All Your Elements on the Table

Complete this worksheet after you have finished reading Chapter 12, Section 2.
You can tell a lot about the properties of an element just by looking at the element's location on the periodic table. This worksheet will help you better understand the connection between the periodic table and the properties of the elements. Follow the directions below, and use crayons or colored pencils to color the periodic table at the bottom of the page.

1. Color the square for hydrogen yellow.

2. Color the groups with very reactive metals red.

3. Color and label the noble gases orange.

4. Color the transition metals green.

5. Using black, mark the zigzag line that shows the position of the metalloids.

6. Color the metalloids purple.

7. Use blue to color all of the nonmetals that are not noble gases.

8. Color the metals in Groups 13–16 brown.

9. Circle and label the actinides in yellow.

10. Circle and label the lanthanides in red.

11. Circle and label the alkali metals in blue.

12. Circle and label the alkaline-earth metals in purple.

13. Circle and label the halogens in green.

REINFORCEMENT & VOCABULARY REVIEW WORKSHEETS   **39**

Name _____ Date _____ Class _____

Bringing It to the Periodic Table

Complete the following puzzle after you finish reading Chapter 12. On the next page is a partially filled-in quotation by Dmitri Mendeleev. Fill in the term described by each clue below. Then put the numbered letters into the corresponding squares on the next page to find out what Mendeleev said. The answers to questions 9–11 are chemical symbols.

1. states that the properties of elements are periodic functions of their atomic numbers
P E R I O D I C   L A W
59 16 27 40 24 / 41

2. column or family in the periodic table
G R O U P
19 35 58

3. any element in Groups 3–12
T R A N S I T I O N   M E T A L
31 14 43 55 18 / 7 33 10

4. elements in Group 1
A L K A L I   M E T A L S
17 14 48 8 36 / 11

5. having a regular, repeating pattern
P E R I O D I C
52 15 25 28 23

6. metals with two electrons in the outer energy level
A L K A L I N E - E A R T H
51 50 20 42 54 2

7. a row of elements
P E R I O D
61 6 26 56

8. elements that don't react readily with other elements
N O B L E   G A S E S
29 49 62 44 64

9. atomic number 9
F
13

10. atomic number 39
Y
57

11. atomic number 54
X E
47 63

Name _____ Date _____ Class _____

Bringing It to the Periodic Table, continued

12. elements having properties of metals and nonmetals
M E T A L L O I D S
39 46 37 5 12

13. the first row of transition metals at the bottom of the periodic table
L A N T H A N I D E S
1 9 34 4

14. the most abundant element in the universe
H Y D R O G E N
21 38 3

15. group containing iodine and chlorine
H A L O G E N S
32 60 30 53 45

Mendeleev's Quotation:

T H E _ E L E M E N T S , I F
1 2 3 _ 4 5 6 7 8 9 10 11 _ 12 13

A R R A N G E D _ A C C O R D I N G _ T O
14 15 16 17 18 19 20 21 _ 22 23 24 25 26 27 28 29 30

T H E I R _ A T O M I C _ W E I G H T S
31 32 33 34 35 _ 36 37 38 39 40 _ 41 42 43 44 45

E X H I B I T _ A _ P E R I O D I C I T Y
46 47 48 49 50 51 _ 52 _ 53 54 55 56 57

O F _ P R O P E R T I E S .
58 _ 59 60 61 62 63 64

*Note to the Teacher:
You may want to inform your students that the term "atomic weight" was used interchangeably with "atomic mass" in the past. "Atomic mass" is the currently accepted term, and is therefore used in this book.

CHAPTER

13 REINFORCEMENT WORKSHEET

Is It an Ion?

Complete this worksheet after you finish reading Chapter 13, Section 2.

Answer the following questions based on the accompanying models. Protons are shown in gray, neutrons are shown in white, and electrons are shown in black.

Answer Questions 1–6 based on Figure 1.

1. How many protons are shown? ___17___

2. In the periodic table, elements are ordered by atomic number, the number of protons in an atom's nucleus. Using the periodic table in your textbook, identify the element shown.

___chlorine___

3. How many electrons are shown? ___18___

4. How many electrons are in the outermost energy level? ___8___

5. If the number of electrons equals the number of protons, then there is no charge, and the model shows a neutral atom. If the numbers are not equal, then you have an ion. Use this reasoning to determine if Figure 1 shows an ion or a neutral atom.

___Figure 1 shows an ion.___

6. To determine a particle's charge, you must compare the number of protons with the number of electrons. Use the spaces to the right to subtract the number of electrons from the number of protons. (Remember, if the number of electrons is greater than the number of protons, the charge will be negative.)

Number of protons	17
Number of electrons –	18
Charge of model	–1

Answer Questions 7–11 based on Figure 2.

7. How many protons are shown? ___10___

8. What element is it? ___neon___

9. How many electrons are shown? ___10___

10. How many electrons are in the outermost energy level? ___8___

11. Is this an ion? If it is, calculate and record the charge.

___No, this is not an ion because it has equal numbers of electrons___
___and protons. It has no charge.___

Figure 1

Figure 2

CHAPTER

13 REINFORCEMENT WORKSHEET

Interview with an Electron

Complete this worksheet after you finish reading Chapter 13, Section 2.

The following descriptions are from the point of view of electrons that are participating in three different types of bonds—ionic, metallic, and covalent. Identify the type of bond that each electron describes. At the bottom of the page is a list of characteristics of bonds and substances containing the bonds. Match each characteristic with the corresponding bond, and write the characteristic in the space provided.

1. My buddies and I do not feel bound to the energy level of one atom in particular, so we can swim freely throughout the substance.

Type of bond: ___This electron describes a metallic bond.___

Characteristics: ___Substances are good conductors of electricity.___

___There's an attraction of positive ions and free-moving electrons.___

2. I might change sides at the start, but once I end up on one side or the other I stick to my decision.

Type of bond: ___This electron describes an ionic bond.___

Characteristics: ___Compounds have a crystal-lattice structure. A metal___

___reacts with a nonmetal. There is a transfer of electrons.___

3. I do not feel partial to either of the atoms in my bond. To be fair, the other bonding electron and I divide our time between the bonded atoms.

Type of bond: ___This electron describes a covalent bond.___

Characteristics: ___There's an attraction between nuclei and shared___

___electrons. Two or more nonmetals are involved.___

Characteristics

- Compounds have a crystal-lattice structure.
- Substances are good conductors of electric current.
- There's an attraction between nuclei and shared electrons.

- There's a transfer of electrons.
- Two or more nonmetals are involved.
- There's an attraction of positive ions and free-moving electrons.
- A metal reacts with a nonmetal.

Name _____ Date _____ Class _____

VOCABULARY REVIEW WORKSHEET

Bonding Puzzle

After completing Chapter 13, give this puzzle a try!
Fill in the blanks in the clues below. Then use the clues to complete the puzzle on the next page.

Clues

1. An arrangement of ions bonded in a repeating three-dimensional pattern is a ____crystal lattice____.

2. A positive particle in the nucleus that attracts electrons is a ____proton____.

3. A unifying explanation for a broad range of hypotheses and observations that have been supported by testing is called a ____theory____.

4. The force of attraction that holds two atoms together is called a(n) ____chemical bond____.

5. An electron in the outermost energy level of an atom is called a ____valence electron____.

6. The force of attraction between oppositely charged ions is a(n) ____ionic bond____.

7. The ____periodic table____ is a chart that displays all elements by atomic number, and can be used to determine the number of valence electrons for some elements.

8. A ____diatomic element____ is an element composed of molecules consisting of two atoms of that element.

9. The joining of atoms to form new substances is called ____chemical bonding____.

10. The force of attraction between the nuclei of atoms and the shared electrons is called a(n) ____covalent bond____.

11. A ____molecule____ is a neutral group of atoms held together by covalent bonds.

12. The force of attraction between a positively charged metal ion and the electrons in a metal is called a(n) ____metallic bond____.

13. A(n) ____ion____ is a charged particle that forms when one or more valence electrons are transferred from one atom to another.

Name _____ Date _____ Class _____

Bonding Puzzle, continued

P	T	E	A	R	B	I	L	O	E	O	M	I	D	C	I	A
T	C	H	E	M	I	C	A	L	B	O	N	D	I	N	G	T
O	N	R	Y	B	O	N	T	M	L	I	C	E	D	N	O	I
L	O	E	Y	E	C	M	E	E	N	T	C	H	N	E	M	I
C	R	A	M	S	B	L	C	B	O	I	N	D	O	N	D	G
M	T	T	E	E	T	U	A	I	O	N	I	C	B	O	N	D
C	C	R	T	Y	L	A	S	T	A	L	L	C	L	M	O	L
E	E	C	A	E	N	E	L	L	A	V	L	I	A	O	B	L
P	L	R	L	O	C	T	C	L	N	T	H	C	E	T	O
R	E	Y	L	O	C	H	E	I	A	O	T	Y	I	A	N	M
I	E	C	I	O	C	B	O	N	M	T	R	C	M	A	E	L
B	C	I	O	N	D	V	P	R	O	T	I	E	N	L	B
D	N	O	B	M	E	T	A	L	E	R	T	I	H	C	A	E
M	E	T	O	L	I	C	I	H	A	P	L	A	C	E	V	N
E	L	E	N	E	N	M	T	C	E	E	L	E	I	E	O	C
T	A	R	D	O	N	S	I	B	O	O	N	D	I	D	C	C
M	V	O	L	E	B	A	T	C	I	D	O	I	R	E	P

Name _____ Date _____ Class _____

CHAPTER
14 REINFORCEMENT WORKSHEET

Activation Energy

Complete this worksheet after you finish reading Chapter 14, Section 3.

Activation energy is the energy a reaction needs to get started. At the bottom of the page are two energy diagrams—one for an exothermic reaction and one for an endothermic reaction. Follow the directions below to label the energy diagrams.

1. In an exothermic reaction, the chemical energy of the reactants is greater than the chemical energy of the products. Write *Exothermic reaction* under the appropriate energy diagram.

2. In an endothermic reaction, the chemical energy of the reactants is lower than the chemical energy of the products. Write *Endothermic reaction* under the appropriate energy diagram.

3. Exothermic reactions give off energy. The energy given off is the difference between the energy of the reactants and the energy of the products. Label the energy given off on the exothermic-energy diagram by writing *Energy given off* in the appropriate space.

4. Endothermic reactions absorb energy. The energy absorbed by a chemical reaction is the difference between the energy of the products and the energy of the reactants. Label the energy absorbed on the endothermic energy diagram by writing *Energy absorbed* in the appropriate space.

5. The activation energy is the energy needed to start a chemical reaction. On the diagrams below, the chemical reaction begins at the top of the peak. The activation energy is the difference between the top of the peak and the energy of the reactants. Label the activation energy of each graph by writing *Activation energy* in the appropriate space.

Energy Diagrams for an Endothermic and an Exothermic Reaction

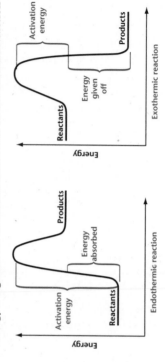

48 HOLT SCIENCE AND TECHNOLOGY

Name _____ Date _____ Class _____

CHAPTER
14 REINFORCEMENT WORKSHEET

Fabulous Food Reactions

Complete this worksheet after you finish reading Chapter 14, Section 2.

In your textbook, you read how dancers can model different chemical reactions. Another way to model chemical reactions is to use food. In the spaces provided, write the type of chemical reaction that is modeled in situations 1–4 below. The possible chemical reactions are *synthesis, decomposition, single-replacement,* and *double-replacement.* Then answer question 5.

1. One day, Oriana packed a ham-on-wheat sandwich, and her friend, Macha, packed a salami-on-rye sandwich. At lunch, they decided to trade meats. Oriana ate a salami-on-wheat sandwich, while Macha ate a ham-on-rye sandwich.

double-replacement reaction
_____

2. Yasu went to an Italian restaurant. When asked for his order he said, "I'd like the Pasta Extravaganza, but could I have meatball sauce instead of the alfredo sauce?"

single-replacement reaction
_____

3. Tara ordered a side order of mixed vegetables with her meal. But before eating them, she separated the vegetables into separate portions of peas and carrots.

decomposition reaction
_____

4. Kevin went to a salad bar. He used lettuce and tomatoes to make his salad.

synthesis reaction
_____

5. Hydrogen and oxygen combine to form water. How is this similar to one of the situations given above?

When hydrogen and oxygen combine to form water, it is a synthesis
_____

reaction—two substances combine to form a new substance. This is like
_____

the salad bar situation above, in which two foods are combined to form a
_____

new food—a salad.
_____

Name _____ Date _____ Class _____

A Reactionary Puzzle

After reading Chapter 14, give this puzzle a try!
Fill in the blanks in the clues below. Then use the clues to complete the puzzle on the next page.

1. A number written below and to the right of a chemical symbol in a formula is called a ___subscript___ .

2. In a ___double___ -replacement reaction, ions in two compounds switch places.

3. The ___activation___ energy is the minimum amount of energy required for substances to react.

4. A chemical ___reaction___ is the process by which one or more substances undergo change to produce one or more different substances.

5. The law of ___conservation___ of ___mass___ states that mass cannot be created or destroyed in ordinary chemical or physical changes. A similar law holds true for ___energy___ .

6. In a ___decomposition___ reaction, a single compound breaks down to form two or more simpler substances.

7. In ___exothermic___ reactions energy is released, and in ___endothermic___ reactions energy is absorbed.

8. In a ___synthesis___ reaction, two or more substances combine to form a single compound.

9. A chemical ___formula___ describes a substance using chemical symbols and numbers.

10. A number written to the left of a chemical symbol or formula is called a ___coefficient___ .

11. In a ___single___ -replacement reaction, one element replaces another that is part of a compound.

12. A chemical ___equation___ is a shorthand description of a chemical reaction.

13. In a chemical reaction, each starting material is a ___reactant___ , and each new substance formed is a ___product___ .

14. A ___catalyst___ speeds up a reaction, and an ___inhibitor___ slows down a reaction.

Name _____ Date _____ Class _____

A Reactionary Puzzle, continued

How many chapter concepts can you find in the block of letters below? Use the clues to help you find them. Words may appear horizontally, vertically, or diagonally.

D	C	Q	R	E	A	C	T	A	N	T	B	Y	C
C	E	X	O	T	H	E	R	M	I	C	G	A	O
D	O	C	A	T	A	L	Y	S	T	R	E	K	E
S	T	N	O	R	V	P	I	T	E	J	I	A	F
U	F	V	S	M	N	S	I	N	G	L	E	C	F
B	O	U	Y	E	P	X	E	H	J	E	R	T	I
S	R	F	N	Q	R	O	Q	I	Q	Q	E	I	C
C	M	J	T	O	V	S	B	Z	U	A	V	I	V
R	U	O	H	O	D	M	A	I	P	A	C	A	E
I	L	R	E	S	U	F	G	T	T	T	I	I	T
P	A	I	S	A	C	I	F	O	R	D	O	O	G
T	U	A	I	K	T	A	U	R	D	O	O	N	D
F	M	H	S	D	O	U	B	L	E	N	N	Q	N
E	N	D	O	T	H	E	R	M	I	C	Q	N	K

CHAPTER 15 VOCABULARY REVIEW WORKSHEET

Compounding the Problem

Use the clues below and on the next page to identify vocabulary terms from Chapter 15. Then find and circle each term in the word search puzzle on the next page.

1. Many fuels are made of these organic compounds.
   _____ hydrocarbons

2. Atoms share electrons in _____ covalent compounds.

3. _____ Nucleic acids are sometimes called the "blueprints of life."

4. The measure of the concentration of hydronium ions in a solution is known as _____ pH.

5. Plants tend to store these as oils. _____ lipids

6. The positive ion of a base and the negative ion of an acid combine to form this ionic compound. _____ salt

7. This substance increases the number of H⁺ when dissolved in water. _____ acid

8. _____ Biochemicals are organic compounds made by living things.

9. This substance is slippery and bitter. _____ base

10. These biochemicals are composed of one or more simple sugar molecules bonded together. _____ carbohydrates

11. These compounds contain oppositely charged ions arranged in a crystal lattice. _____ ionic

12. These compounds are composed of molecules whose carbon atoms are arranged in a straight chain, a branched chain, or a ring _____ organic

13. _____ Proteins are biochemicals that have many functions, such as regulating chemical activities.

14. This special paper is used to test for acids and bases. _____ litmus

15. The building blocks of proteins are _____ amino acids

16. This protein regulates the amount of glucose in your blood. _____ insulin

---

A Simple Solution, continued

ACIDS

taste sour

may be corrosive

react with baking soda to produce carbon dioxide gas

change blue litmus to red

pH less than 7

found in vinegar

excess hydronium ions

found in orange juice

H⁺

BASES

taste bitter

may be corrosive

excess hydroxide ions

found in drain cleaner

pH greater than 7

used to make soap

slippery

OH⁻

change red litmus to blue

neutralize lakes with low pH

SOAP

SALTS

form from the reaction of a metal and a nonmetal

sodium chloride

formed from a neutralization reaction

used in plasterboard

used to de-ice roads

Name _____ Date _____ Class _____

CHAPTER 16 ▸ REINFORCEMENT WORKSHEET

The Decay of a Nucleus

Complete this worksheet after you finish reading Chapter 16, Section 1.
Fill in the blanks in items 1–4, and then complete the table at the bottom of the page.

1. An alpha particle is the same as the nucleus of an atom of the element ___helium___. It contains ___two___ neutron(s) and ___two___ proton(s).

2. During alpha decay, the atomic number decreases by ___two___ and the mass number ___decreases___ by four.

3. In one type of beta decay, a neutron in a radioactive nucleus breaks down into a ___proton___ and a(n) ___electron___.

4. When a radioactive nucleus releases a beta particle, its atomic number increases by one, and the mass number ___stays the same___.
(decreases, stays the same, or increases)

In the text, you learned that a uranium-238 nucleus undergoes 14 decays to become lead-206. Now you can construct a decay series by completing the table below. You will need the periodic table of the elements. The first two steps have been done for you. (Hint: All beta particles released in this series are electrons, not positrons.)

Step	Type of decay	New atomic number	New mass number	Name of isotope formed
1	Alpha	92	238	U-238
2	Beta	90	234	Th-234
3	Beta	91	234	Pa-234
4	Alpha	92	234	U-234
5	Alpha	90	230	Th-230
6	Alpha	88	226	Ra-226
7	Alpha	86	222	Rn-222
8	Alpha	84	218	Po-218
9	Beta	82	214	Pb-214
10	Beta	83	214	Bi-214
11	Alpha	84	214	Po-214
12	Beta	82	210	Pb-210
13	Beta	83	210	Bi-210
14	Alpha	82	206	Pb-206

Name _____ Date _____ Class _____

Compounding the Problem, continued

17. This type of carbohydrate, found in bread, cereal, and pasta, is called a ___complex___ carbohydrate.

18. This substance changes color in the presence of an acid or a base. ___indicator___

19. A carbon atom can form no more than this number of bonds. ___four___

20. This type of nucleic acid is the genetic material of the cell. ___DNA___

21. This type of hydrocarbon contains carbon atoms connected only by single bonds. ___saturated___

22. ___Hemoglobin___ is a protein that carries oxygen to all parts of your body.

Word search grid:

```
Y  X  B  H  T  A  R  O  T  A  C  I  D  N  I  A
J  C  E  I  P  N  X  A  B  R  M  W  S  O  N  L
A  H  I  L  O  T  E  I  O  B  I  A  E  D  I  T
S  W  L  N  P  C  L  P  D  I  L  S  C  P  I  L
N  S  R  A  A  M  H  A  K  X  A  A  I  N  Y  N
O  D  S  C  G  G  O  E  S  B  R  D  I  D  C  I
B  I  N  K  A  A  R  C  M  B  S  L  M  V  H  B
R  C  I  Z  V  U  U  O  I  U  W  N  U  P  O  L
A  A  E  J  O  E  Y  H  C  S  C  Q  P  H  G  L
C  O  T  F  A  E  Y  O  N  A  L  A  E  T  X  G
O  N  O  V  W  D  V  I  H  C  I  L  I  G  O
R  R  L  R  A  I  X  Y  F  M  I  T  S  Q  M
D  M  P  A  L  O  J  K  V  K  K  T  D  M  H  E
Y  A  T  E  N  G  L  V  P  B  E  D  U  Q  U  H
H  E  N  I  N  B  D  E  T  A  R  U  T  A  S  S
S  T  C  N  U  C  L  E  I  C  A  C  I  D  S  R
```

CHAPTER 16

REINFORCEMENT WORKSHEET

Fission or Fusion?

Complete this worksheet after you finish reading Chapter 16, Section 2.

While it's true that fusion and fission are both types of nuclear reactions, the similarity ends there. Follow the steps below to sort out the facts and eliminate any con-*fusion*!

1. Take a look at the illustrations in the table below. In the first column, label each illustration either "fusion" or "fission."

2. Read over the following list of information. Then write each piece of information next to the appropriate type of nuclear reaction. Answers may be used more than once.

- Chernobyl
- not currently used to provide electrical energy
- hydrogen is a plasma
- fuels 20 percent of the electrical energy used in the United States
- requires temperatures over 100,000,000°C
- radioactive waste products

- occurs in the sun's core
- no radioactive waste products
- energy is released
- large nucleus splits into two smaller nuclei
- uranium
- two or more nuclei join together to form a more-massive nucleus

Nuclear Reaction Chart

fission	Chernobyl fuels 20 percent of the electrical energy used in the United States radioactive waste products energy is released large nucleus splits into two smaller nuclei uranium
fusion	not currently used to provide electrical energy hydrogen is a plasma requires temperatures over 100,000,000°C occurs in the sun's core no radioactive waste products energy is released two or more nuclei join together to form a more-massive nucleus

---

CHAPTER 16

VOCABULARY REVIEW WORKSHEET

Atomic Energy Acrostic

After you finish Chapter 16, give this puzzle a try!
Fill in the blanks below. Then put letters into the matching numbered squares to reveal a quote by Marie Curie.

1. occurs when two or more small nuclei join together to form a larger, more-massive nucleus

   N U C L E A R   F U S I O N
   $\overline{20}$ $\overline{38}$ $\overline{9}$

2. decay that occurs when a nucleus releases a positron or an electron

   B E T A
   $\overline{13}$

3. the ability of the nuclei of some atoms to give off high-energy particles and rays

   R A D I O A C T I V I T Y
   $\overline{23}$ $\overline{2}$ $\overline{16}$ $\overline{5}$ $\overline{27}$

4. the collective name of high-energy particles and rays given off by the nuclei of atoms

   N U C L E A R   R A D I A T I O N
   $\overline{42}$ $\overline{40}$ $\overline{3}$ $\overline{30}$

5. the process by which high-energy particles and rays are released

   R A D I O A C T I V E   D E C A Y
   $\overline{25}$ $\overline{46}$ $\overline{34}$ $\overline{19}$ $\overline{47}$ $\overline{37}$ $\overline{33}$

6. atoms with the same number of protons but different numbers of neutrons

   I S O T O P E S
   $\overline{15}$ $\overline{2}$ $\overline{16}$ $\overline{41}$

7. occurs when a large nucleus splits, releasing energy and two smaller nuclei

   N U C L E A R   F I S S I O N
   $\overline{11}$ $\overline{43}$ $\overline{35}$ $\overline{6}$

8. the sum of protons and neutrons in an atom

   M A S S   N U M B E R
   $\overline{22}$ $\overline{29}$ $\overline{1}$ $\overline{36}$

9. high-energy light waves that are released from a radioactive nucleus during alpha decay and beta decay

   G A M M A   R A Y S
   $\overline{7}$

Name _____ Date _____ Class _____

Atomic Energy Acrostic, continued

10. the length of time it takes for one-half of the nuclei of a radioactive isotope to decay

H A L F - L I F E
‾32‾ ‾ ‾ ‾28‾ ‾12‾ ‾24‾

11. occurs when a nucleus releases a particle consisting of two protons and two neutrons

A L P H A   D E C A Y
‾10‾ ‾ ‾ ‾ ‾4‾   ‾ ‾ ‾ ‾ ‾

12. the isotope often used to determine the age of once-living things

C A R B O N -14
‾ ‾18‾ ‾17‾ ‾ ‾

13. a continuous series of nuclear fission reactions

N U C L E A R   C H A I N
‾ ‾ ‾ ‾ ‾44‾ ‾14‾   ‾ ‾ ‾ ‾26‾ ‾39‾

R E A C T I O N
‾21‾ ‾ ‾ ‾ ‾ ‾ ‾31‾

What Marie Curie said:

N	O	T	H	I	N	G		I	N		L	I	F	E
1	2	3	4	5	6	7		8	9		10	11	12	13

I	S		T	O	
14	15		16	17	

B	E		F	E	A	R	E	D	,	
18	19		20	21	22	23	24	25		

I	T		I	S		O	N	L	Y	
26	27		28	29		30	31	32	33	

T	O		B	E	
34	35		36	37	

U	N	D	E	R	S	T	O	O	D	.
38	39	40	41	42	43	44	45	46	47	

Name _____ Date _____ Class _____

CHAPTER 17 — REINFORCEMENT WORKSHEET

Charge!

Complete this worksheet after you have finished reading Chapter 17, Section 1.

There are three ways for an object to gain a charge: friction, conduction, and induction. When it loses its charge it experiences electric discharge. Label the following pictures as examples of *conduction, induction, friction,* or *electric discharge.*

1. _____ electric discharge

2. _____ conduction

3. _____ conduction

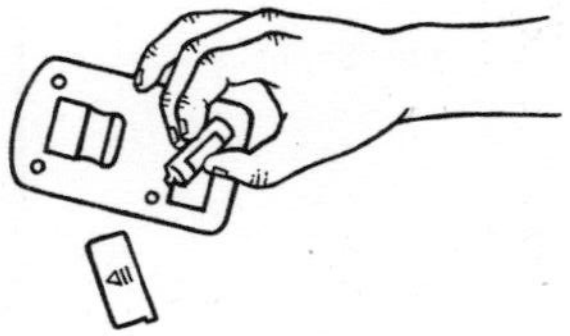

4. _____ induction or friction

5. _____ friction

6. _____ induction

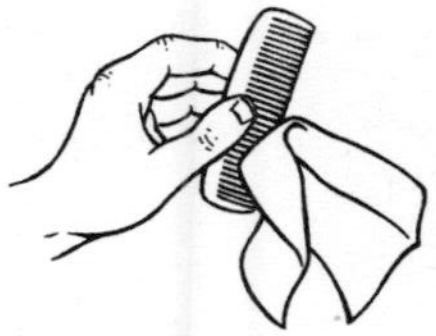

Name _____ Date _____ Class _____

CHAPTER

17 **REINFORCEMENT WORKSHEET**

Electric Circuits

Complete this worksheet after you have finished reading Chapter 17, Section 4.

Two electric circuits powered by cells are shown below. Answer the following questions based on the information given in the diagrams. Questions 1–6 refer to Figure 1, and Questions 8–12 refer to Figure 2.

Label the parts of the circuit and the cell by writing the letter that corresponds to the appropriate part in the space provided.

Figure 1

1. _A_ load
2. _D_ electrode
3. _B_ wire
4. _E_ electrolyte
5. _C_ energy source
6. Is this circuit connected in series or in parallel? _____series_____

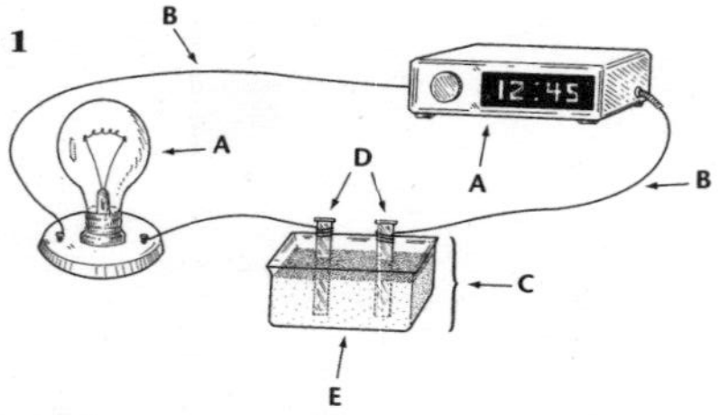

7. A cell that contains liquid electrolytes is called a _____wet_____ cell.

Figure 2

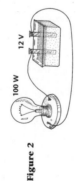

8. What is the power in this circuit? _____100 W_____

9. What is the voltage in this circuit? _____12 V_____

10. Recall that $I = P/V$. If you divide the power of the circuit by its voltage, you'll get the circuit's current. What is the current of this circuit?

The current is 8.33 amperes.

11. Remember that Ohm's law can be rearranged to say: $R = V/I$. If you divide the circuit's voltage by its current, you'll get the resistance of the circuit. What is the resistance caused by the light bulb?

The resistance is 1.44 ohms.

12. This cell contains a solid electrolyte, so it is a _____dry_____ cell.

Name _____ Date _____ Class _____

An Electrifying Puzzle, continued

[Crossword puzzle with answers:]
- INSULATOR
- PARALLEL
- CURRENT
- POTENTIAL
- CHARGE
- LOAD
- INDUCTION
- THERMOCOUPLE
- BATTERY
- CIRCUIT
- RESISTANCE
- SWITCH
- CONDUCTOR

Name _____ Date _____ Class _____

CHAPTER 18

REINFORCEMENT WORKSHEET

Planet Lodestone

Complete this worksheet after reading Chapter 18, Section 1.

After months in space, Captain Iva Braveheart and her crew are approaching their destination—the planet Lodestone. Read the following entries in Captain Braveheart's personal spacelog, and answer the questions.

Earth date July 21, 2313

Finally, we are drawing near to the planet Lodestone. Tomorrow we should be close enough to perform some tests on the planet. I am most curious to know what the planet's core is like—and whether compasses are likely to work on this planet.

1. What properties of planet Lodestone's core would indicate that the planet probably has magnetic properties?

Sample answer: If the planet had a liquid core that contained mostly iron

and nickel, like Earth's, then the planet would probably have magnetic

properties.

Earth date July 22, 2313

Our tests indicate that the planet should have magnetic poles, just like Earth. A small team will visit the planet's surface tomorrow. I'm going to take along a bar magnet and string to find magnetic north and south on Lodestone.

2. How will the captain find magnetic north and south on this planet using a bar magnet and string?

Sample answer: When a bar magnet is suspended on a string in a magnetic

field, the magnet will always point in the same direction. The north pole

of the magnet will point to the south magnetic pole of the planet.

3. Captain Braveheart plans to name geographic North on planet Lodestone after magnetic north and geographic South after magnetic south. If she does, will North and South be the same on Lodestone as they are on Earth? Explain.

Sample answer: No; on Earth, geographic North is really a magnetic south

pole and geographic South is really a magnetic north pole. So a magnet that

points north on Lodestone would point south on Earth.

Name _____ Date _____ Class _____

CHAPTER 18

REINFORCEMENT WORKSHEET

A Magnetic Time

Complete this worksheet after reading Chapter 18, Section 3.

1. Draw a line from the person or group of people in Column A to their contribution to the study of electromagnetism in Column B. Be careful; two scientists match with one contribution.

2. Draw a line from the contribution in Column B to the year or time period when it occurred in Column C.

Column A	Column B	Column C
Hans Christian Oersted	proposed that the Earth is one giant magnet	2,000 years ago
Michael Faraday	found a mineral called magnetite, which attracts iron-containing objects	1831
Greeks	found that a changing magnetic field could induce an electric current	1600
William Gilbert	after many experiments, concluded that an electric current produces a magnetic field	1820
Joseph Henry		

3. Use the information above to create a timeline in the space below.

Sample answer: The Development of Electromagnetism

AD 0 — 1600 — 1810 — 1820 — 1830 — 1840 — 1850 — 1820

- Greeks find magnetite.
- Gilbert proposes Earth is a giant magnet.
- Oersted finds that an electric current produces a magnetic field.
- Faraday and Henry find that a changing magnetic field induces an electric current.

CHAPTER 19

REINFORCEMENT WORKSHEET

Semiconductors' Conductivity

Complete this worksheet after reading Chapter 19, Section 1.

A semiconductor is a material that conducts electrical energy better than an insulator but not as well as a conductor. Silicon may be the most well-known semiconductor, but it's not the only one. Another semiconductor is germanium (Ge). Use the periodic table in your textbook to help you answer the following questions.

1. Like silicon, germanium has ___4___ electrons in the outermost energy level of each atom.

Doping a semiconductor means replacing a few atoms of the semiconductor with a few atoms of another substance that has a different number of valence electrons.

2. Germanium can be doped with antimony (Sb), a group ___15___ element, which has ___5___ electrons in the outermost energy level of each atom.

3. Germanium can be doped with indium (In), a group ___13___ element, which has ___3___ electrons in the outermost energy level of each atom.

4. In the space below, sketch the arrangement of electrons in pure germanium, in germanium doped with antimony, and in germanium doped with indium. Draw only the electrons in the outermost energy levels. The outermost energy level of each atom is represented by a gray circle.

germanium

germanium-antimony

germanium-indium

An n-type semiconductor is a doped semiconductor with an "extra" electron. A p-type semiconductor is a doped semiconductor with a "hole" where an electron could be.

5. Doping germanium with ___antimony___ results in an n-type semiconductor.

6. Doping germanium with ___indium___ results in a p-type semiconductor.

A Puzzling Transformation, continued

1. M A G N E T I C   F O R C E

2. P O L E S

3. G A L V A N O M E T E R

4. E L E C T R I C   M O T O R

5. E L E C T R O M A G N E T

6. O E R S T E D

7. I N D U C T I O N

8. F E R R O M A G N E T

9. F A R A D A Y

10. M A G L E V

11. D O M A I N

12. M A G N E T I C   F I E L D

13. G E N E R A T O R

14. S O L E N O I D

15. T R A N S F O R M E R

16. M A G N E T

Name _____ Date _____ Class _____

A Circuit-ous Crossword, continued

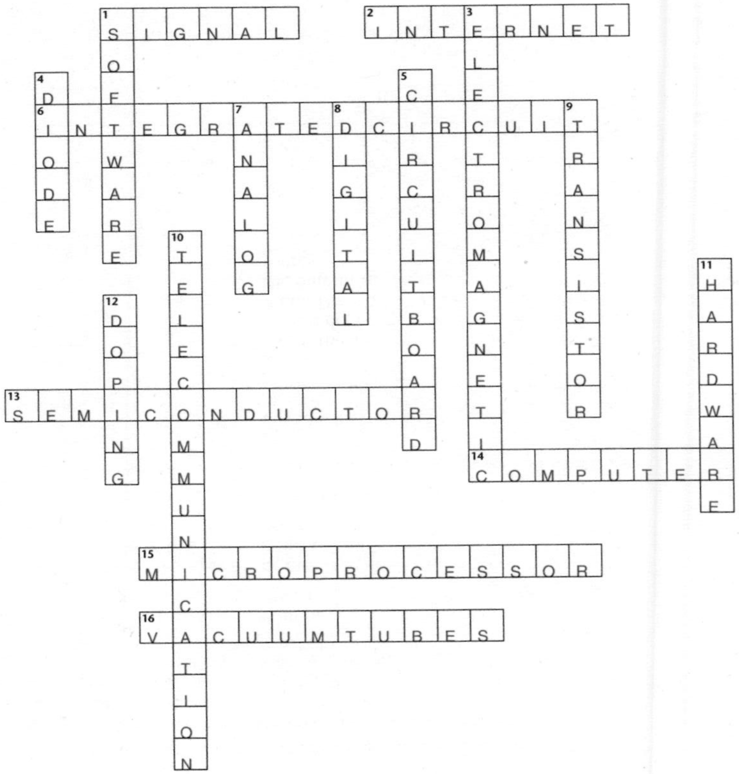

(crossword puzzle grid with answers)

Across/Down answers shown in grid:
1. SIGNAL
2. INTERNET
3. TELEVISION (partial)
4. DIODE
5. CIRCUIT
6. RADIO
7. INTEGRATED CIRCUIT
8. TRANSISTOR
9. TRANSISTOR
10. TELECOMMUNICATION
11. HARDWARE
12. DIODE
13. SEMICONDUCTOR
14. COMPUTER
15. MICROPROCESSOR
16. VACUUM TUBES

Name _____ Date _____ Class _____

CHAPTER
19 REINFORCEMENT WORKSHEET

The Ins and Outs of Computing

Complete this worksheet after you finish Chapter 19, Section 3.
Fill in the blanks in the paragraph below with the terms *input device, microprocessor, memory,* and *output device.*

1. Information is entered into a computer using a(n) _input device_. The information is processed by the central processing unit, which is a(n) _microprocessor_, or the information is stored in the computer's _memory_ until it is needed. When a computer finishes a task, it shows the results on a(n) _output device_.

2. Below is an illustration of a desktop computer setup. Label the parts of the computer with the following terms: *speaker, monitor, keyboard, mouse, floppy disk, printer.*

3. Using colored pencils or crayons, color input devices yellow, output devices red, and storage and processing devices blue.

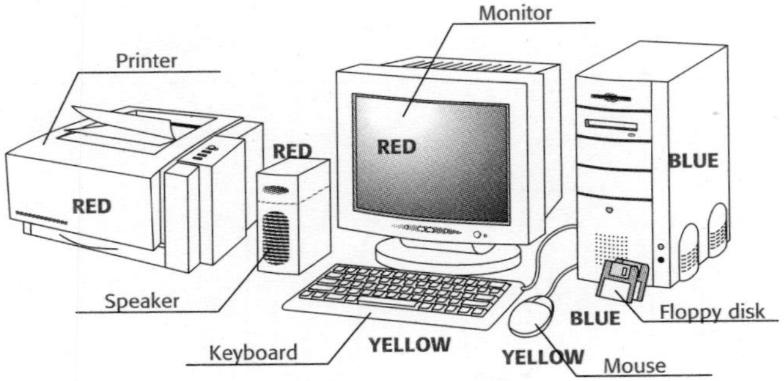

(Illustration labels: Printer — RED; Monitor — RED; BLUE; RED; BLUE; Floppy disk; Mouse — YELLOW; Keyboard — YELLOW; Speaker — RED)

4. The computer shown above does not have a modem. If it did, what color would you shade the modem? Explain.
   Sample answer: A modem can be an input device (yellow) and an output device (red), so I would shade the modem orange.

Name _____ Date _____ Class _____

REINFORCEMENT WORKSHEET

Getting on the Same Frequency

Complete this worksheet after you finish reading Chapter 20, Section 2. Examine the diagram below, and then answer the questions that follow.

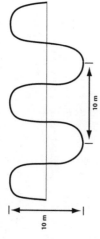

1. What is the amplitude of the wave?

   The amplitude of the wave is 5 m.

2. What is the wavelength?

   The wavelength is 10 m.

Remember, frequency, expressed in hertz (Hz), is the number of waves produced in a given amount of time.

3. If you were watching this wave go by and counted five crests passing a certain point in 5 seconds, what would be the frequency of the wave? Use the formula and the space below to calculate your answer.

$$\text{Frequency} = \frac{\text{number of waves}}{\text{time}} = \frac{5}{5 \text{ s}} = \frac{1}{\text{s}} = 1 \text{ Hz}$$

4. What would the frequency of the wave be if you counted 10 crests in five seconds? Use the space below to calculate the answer.

$$\text{Frequency} = \frac{10}{5 \text{ s}} = 2 \text{ Hz}$$

5. If the wavelength became 12 m but the wave speed remained the same, would the frequency increase, decrease, or stay the same?

   If the wavelength became 12 m, the frequency would decrease.

Name _____ Date _____ Class _____

REINFORCEMENT WORKSHEET

Makin' Waves

Complete this worksheet after you finish reading Chapter 20, Section 3. Diagram and label the interaction described below, and then answer the questions that follow.

Wave A, with an amplitude of 3 m, meets wave B, with an amplitude of 3 m. When A and B overlap, the wave produced (C) has an amplitude of 6 m.

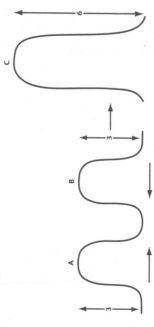

1. What type of wave interaction is described? Explain.

   Sample answer: The wave interaction is constructive interference because when the waves overlapped, the amplitude of the resulting wave (C) was greater than the amplitude of the individual waves.

2. If wave A were to overlap with a different wave to produce a new wave that had an amplitude of 0 m instead of 6 m, would this be the same type of interaction described above? Explain.

   Sample answer: No; if the amplitude of the resulting wave were 0 m, the amplitude of the resulting wave would be less than the amplitude of the original waves. This would be an example of total destructive interference.

Name _____ Date _____ Class _____

Copyright © by Holt, Rinehart and Winston. All rights reserved.

CHAPTER 20 **VOCABULARY REVIEW WORKSHEET**

Let's Do the Wave!

After you finish Chapter 20, give this puzzle a try!

Figure out the words described by the clues below, and write each word in the appropriate space. Then find and circle the words in the puzzle on the next page.

1. _medium_ — a substance through which a wave can travel

2. _refraction_ — the bending of a wave as it passes at an angle from one medium to another

3. _wave_ — a disturbance that transmits energy through matter and space

4. _resonance_ — when one vibrating object causes similar vibrations in another object that is nearby

5. _trough_ — the lowest point of a transverse wave

6. _frequency_ — the number of waves produced in a given amount of time

7. _interference_ — when two or more waves overlap

8. _perpendicular_ — describes lines that meet at right angles

9. _reflection_ — an echo, for example (wave interaction)

10. _surface_ — a wave that occurs at the boundary between two media when transverse and longitudinal waves combine

11. _longitudinal_ — wave in which particles in the medium vibrate back and forth along the path the wave travels

12. _transverse_ — waves in which particles of the medium vibrate in an up-and-down motion

13. _wavelength_ — the distance between two adjacent compressions

14. _amplitude_ — the maximum distance a wave vibrates from its rest position

15. _standing_ — kind of wave that looks like it is stationary

16. _crest_ — the highest point of a transverse wave

17. _hertz_ — measurement equal to one wave per second

18. _diffraction_ — the bending of waves around a barrier or through an opening

---

Name _____ Date _____ Class _____

Let's Do the Wave! continued

In the puzzle below, find the words from the blanks on the previous page. Words may appear horizontally, vertically, or diagonally.

S	W	V	O	M	Y	O	Y	S	F	S	U	M	V	J	Z	X
U	B	H	C	P	I	C	E	X	T	S	V	G	T	G	C	R
R	A	L	U	C	I	D	N	E	P	R	E	P	M	N	Z	C
F	G	O	V	W	D	S	R	E	F	L	E	C	T	I	O	N
A	T	N	T	R	W	O	L	F	U	L	O	O	K	D	A	T
C	R	G	E	E	N	O	E	W	M	Q	O	M	I	N	M	L
E	I	A	F	R	N	S	I	N	G	E	R	A	A	B	O	O
I	N	T	E	R	F	E	R	E	N	C	E	R	U	T	T	W
W	S	U	V	A	E	S	E	P	R	S	E	T	F	S	T	A
Y	V	D	O	C	O	L	B	N	O	O	U	L	D	N	M	V
T	E	I	O	T	U	S	N	N	A	Y	A	I	C	P	E	E
T	R	N	O	I	T	C	A	R	F	F	I	D	L	M	D	L
R	S	A	M	O	I	N	R	Y	O	E	L	I	P	N	I	E
O	E	L	J	N	C	A	T	N	D	W	T	O	W	H	U	N
U	E	F	H	E	R	T	Z	L	E	U	R	V	E	B	M	G
G	G	I	L	F	U	N	S	L	D	O	U	C	R	E	S	T
H	C	O	D	I	W	A	V	E	A	T	I	Q	U	O	R	H

CHAPTER 21 VOCABULARY REVIEW WORKSHEET

Sound Puzzle

After you finish reading Chapter 21, give this puzzle a try!
Fill in each blank with the correct term. Then use the vocabulary words to find the words in the puzzle on the next page.

1. The apparent change in the pitch of a car's horn as it moves past you is a result of the _____ Doppler _____ effect.

2. When any kind of wave bounces off a barrier, the bouncing back of the wave is called _____ reflection _____. A bounced sound wave is called an _____ echo _____. This kind of sound wave is the basis for _____ echolocation _____, a method whales and bats use to find food.

3. The bending of waves around barriers or through openings is called _____ diffraction _____.

4. Each instrument has a unique _____ quality _____ that is the result of several pitches blending together through interference.

5. The _____ loudness _____ of the note depends on whether it is played softly or loudly, and the _____ pitch _____ is how low or high the note sounds.

6. Due to _____ resonance _____, the vibration of a tuning fork can cause a guitar string to vibrate when the fork is held near the string.

7. The hammer, anvil, and stirrup bones are in the _____ middle _____ ear. The _____ inner _____ ear changes vibrations into electrical signals. The _____ outer _____ ear acts as a funnel for sound waves.

8. Constructive or destructive _____ interference _____ occurs when sound waves overlap and combine.

9. The _____ decibel _____ is a unit used to express how loud or soft a sound is.

10. A _____ noise _____ is an undesirable, nonmusical sound that includes a random mix of pitches.

Doppler Dan's Dump Truck, continued

1. Use your textbook to find the speed of sound in air at 20°C.

   wave speed = ___343 m/s___

2. Doppler Dan bought his horn from Honk, Inc. They guaranteed that the horn will honk at a frequency of 350 Hz. Use the equation on the previous page to calculate the wavelength of sound made by Dan's horn and show your work here.

   (343 m/s) ÷ 350 Hz = 0.98 m

3. Find the wavelength of the sound by measuring the distance from one compression to the next. From where Otis is standing, what is the wavelength of the sound? ___0.90 m___

4. The frequency of sound that you hear is the speed of the sound divided by the wavelength. What frequency did Otis hear?

   (343 m/s) ÷ 0.90 m = 381 Hz

5. What is the wavelength of the sound on the side of the dump truck where Elinor is standing.? ___1.06 m___

6. What frequency did Elinor hear?

   (343 m/s) ÷ 1.06 m = 324 Hz

7. Complete the chart below.

Listener	Sound wavelength	Sound frequency
Dan	0.98 m	350 Hz
Otis	0.90 m	381 Hz
Elinor	1.06 m	324 Hz

8. Now use the information that you have just gathered and your understanding of the Doppler effect to explain why Otis heard the sound differently than Dan.

   As the dump truck moved toward Otis, he heard a higher frequency (higher pitched) sound than Dan. Dan was moving with the sound source, so he heard the actual frequency of the horn.

Name _____ Date _____ Class _____

Sound Puzzle, continued

11. An extremely fast airplane can cause an explosive sound called a _____ sonic _____ boom.

12. _____ Infrasonic _____ sounds have a frequency lower than 20 Hz, while _____ ultrasonic _____ sounds have a frequency higher than 20,000 Hz.

13. In a _____ standing _____ wave, some portions of the wave are at rest while other portions have a large amplitude.

Search the puzzle below to find each of the words you wrote in the blanks above, and circle these words in the puzzle. Words may appear horizontally, vertically, or diagonally.

F	B	O	Z	U	M	H	I	Z	I	Z	E	D
I	Q	U	A	L	I	T	Y	M	N	R	R	I
W	G	T	D	T	O	T	W	F	T	M	E	H
V	B	E	W	R	K	U	R	L	E	V	L	F
R	U	R	X	E	A	D	Z	R	S	P	L	R
X	E	S	T	S	S	H	Y	N	F	U	P	O
E	L	N	Z	O	K	C	C	E	N	O	C	A
F	D	O	N	N	O	I	S	E	R	S	D	C
J	E	I	H	I	O	K	C	Z	E	K	S	T
C	C	V	N	C	P	K	Y	H	N	X	I	I
M	I	N	R	E	F	L	E	C	T	I	O	N
C	B	N	E	M	I	D	D	L	E	T	Y	I
R	E	S	O	N	A	N	C	E	Q	U	I	A
P	L	O	E	S	T	A	N	D	I	N	G	P

Name _____ Date _____ Class _____

Light Interactions

Complete this worksheet after you finish reading Chapter 22, Section 3.

Light waves can interact with objects or with other light waves in a variety of ways. Complete the table by writing a description or explanation and an example of each kind of light interaction. The first example is provided.

Interaction	Description or explanation	Example
Reflection	A wave bounces off an object.	A green sweater looks green because green light is reflected off it.
Absorption	Energy carried by light waves is transferred to particles of matter.	Sample answer: Due to absorption (and scattering), the beam of a flashlight appears dimmer the further it is from the flashlight.
Scattering	Light energy is released by particles of matter that have absorbed energy.	Sample answer: Scattering of blue light makes the sky look blue.
Refraction	The path of a wave bends as it passes at an angle from one medium to another.	Sample answer: A straw placed in a glass of water appears bent.
Diffraction	Diffraction is the bending of waves around barriers and through openings.	Sample answer: Shadows appear slightly blurry at the edges.
Interference	Waves overlap and combine.	Sample answer: When light of one wavelength shines through two slits onto a screen a series of bright and dark bands will appear.

CHAPTER 22 · VOCABULARY REVIEW WORKSHEET

Puzzle of Light

After you finish reading Chapter 22, give this puzzle a try!
Fill in the blanks below. Then put the letters in the matching numbered squares on the next page to reveal a quote by Albert Einstein.

1. the bending of waves as they pass into a different medium

R E F R A C T I O N
8 12 38

2. energy emitted in the form of EM waves

R A D I A T I O N
37 7 20

3. the release of energy by particles of matter that have absorbed extra energy

S C A T T E R I N G
32 11 39

4. the material that gives paint its color by absorbing some colors of light and reflecting others

P I G M E N T
6 22

5. occurs when waves overlap and combine

I N T E R F E R E N C E
34 16

6. the entire range of EM waves, such as light, radio waves, microwaves, and X rays

E L E C T R O M A G N E T I C
35 17 1
S P E C T R U M
31 9

7. the bending of waves around a barrier or through an opening

D I F F R A C T I O N
15 26

8. the passing of light through matter

T R A N S M I S S I O N
13 5 27

9. materials that transmit light easily, without scattering

T R A N S P A R E N T
19 28 33

10. waves that are used in radar

M I C R O W A V E S
18 10

11. can be created by combining red, green, and blue light

W H I T E   L I G H T
2 23 14

CHAPTER 22 · REINFORCEMENT WORKSHEET

Fiona, Private Eye

Complete this worksheet after you finish reading Chapter 22, Section 3.
Fiona wants to be a detective. In order to pass the entrance exam to Private Eye University, she is practicing her spy skills on her friends Jorge, Charles, and Tamika. Reflection is one of the hardest sections on the exam. Use what you have discussed in class to help Fiona learn about the law of reflection.

Figure 1

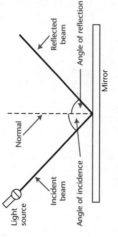

Light source
Incident beam
Angle of incidence
Normal
Reflected beam
Angle of reflection
Mirror

1. Figure 1 in Fiona's notes shows a beam of light hitting and reflecting off a mirror. Label the *normal, incident beam, reflected beam, angle of incidence,* and *angle of reflection* on the diagram.

Fiona knows from the law of reflection that the angle of incidence always equals the angle of reflection. She uses this law to plan a system of mirrors that will allow her to spy on her friends. With her special arrangement of mirrors, Fiona can watch her friends walk by as she hides behind a brick wall.

2. Figure 2 shows the arrangement of mirrors. Using the law of reflection, draw the path of light as it would reflect off each of the mirrors. The normals have been drawn on the reflecting surfaces for you. (Hint: Not all of the mirrors will be used.)

Figure 2

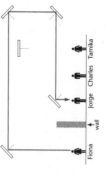

Fiona   wall   Jorge Charles Tamika

3. Which of her friends is Fiona able to see with her mirrors in their current arrangement?

Name _____ Date _____ Class _____

Puzzle of Light, continued

12. the transfer of energy from light waves to particles of matter

A B S O R P T I O N
   3   4   36

13. when a wave bounces off an object

R E F L E C T I O N
 3   24

14. materials that do not transmit any light

O P A Q U E
21   29

15. materials that transmit and scatter light

T R A N S L U C E N T
        25   30

What Albert Einstein said:

T	H	E		I	M	P	O	R	T	A	N	T		T	H	I	N	G
1	2	3		5	6	7	8	9	10	11	12			13	14	15	16	17

I	S		N	O	T		T	O		S	T	O	P
18	19		20	21	22		23	24		25	26	27	28

Q	U	E	S	T	I	O	N	I	N	G	.
29	30	31	32	33	34	35	36	37	38	39	

Name _____ Date _____ Class _____

CHAPTER 23

REINFORCEMENT WORKSHEET

Mirror, Mirror

Complete this worksheet after reading Chapter 23, Section 2.
You will need a straightedge for this activity. Each of the following four illustrations features an object, an image, and a mirror. The optical axis and the focal point are also shown where appropriate.

1. Identify the mirror as plane, convex, or concave. (Circle your answer.)

2. Identify the image as a real or virtual image. (Circle your answer.)

3. For concave and convex mirrors, if the rays are not drawn, draw them into the ray diagram.

plane or convex or concave
real image or virtual image

plane or convex or concave
real image or virtual image

plane or convex or concave
real image or virtual image

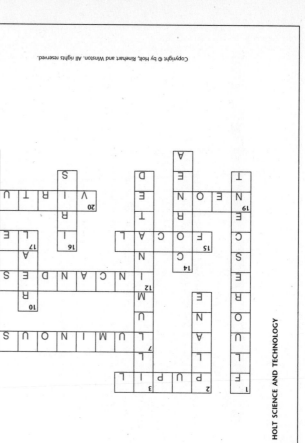

Name _____ Date _____ Class _____

An Enlightening Puzzle, continued

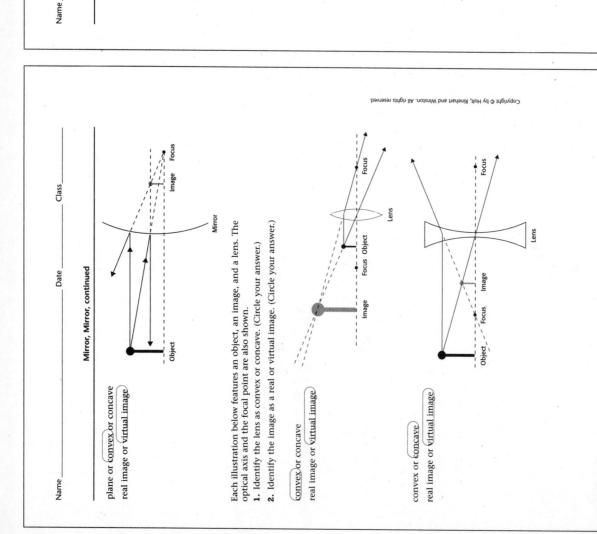

Name _____ Date _____ Class _____

Mirror, Mirror, continued

Each illustration below features an object, an image, and a lens. The optical axis and the focal point are also shown.

1. Identify the lens as convex or concave. (Circle your answer.)
2. Identify the image as a real or virtual image. (Circle your answer.)

plane or convex or concave
real image or virtual image

convex or concave
real image or virtual image

convex or concave
real image or virtual image